FIRE START- ERS

a collection:
noah roselli

firestarters

introduction

first:
picture lady gaga dressed in all white sitting on a horse, singing your favorite song but instead of having a microphone, she has an ice cream cone.
now:
read this in a really high pitched voice like a little squeaking mouse squeaking loudly
and:

READ THIS LIKE I AM YELLING

oh, also:
read this in a british accent. now use a voice as if you were a new yorker from the bronx. or how about the italians and how much they like their mutz. now read this in a german accent. or a canadian accent, eh? or what about an angry girl who says like a lot like this like she just like i do not really like know like always talks like this like she is mad like you know?
did you do it?
if no: STOP WHAT ON EARTH ARE YOU DOING IM YELLING AT YOU AGAIN GO BACK AND REREAD UGH
if yes: thank you, you can read on.

that is why i write: dead trees cut up into fractions of centimeters in height, stained with ink of different colors can have the ability to make you cry, laugh, scream, or think a certain way. like i am writing this on monday february first at eleven thirty-four in the evening and i have school tomorrow but you may be reading this weeks, months, even years after i wrote this and still i have had the ability to cause you to think a certain way.

so now i just want to tell you my story. how and why i began to write. i want you to get familiar with me before you read my thoughts. i have really always enjoyed writing. i would sit in front of this really big desktop that my family had in the basement and i would create stories. but i really found my true calling for writing in fifth and in seventh grade.

okay so fifth grade was a pretty strange year for me. my sister had a bad concussion from playing soccer and i grew depressed but i found support whenever i wrote. i had an assignment for english class that was one of those writing prompts where there is a picture and you have to create a story based solely around that photograph. the picture i received was one of a blood stained column. i wrote a story basically about a detective and i remember being the last person to read it aloud to the class and within the first paragraph of me getting up there and reading, i had people laughing. and i loved that.

fast forward to seventh grade: i took a course where for the first two marking periods i had a class on literature and basically all we did was read books and for the last two we would write. one of the first assignments i had was to write a story about a plane crash. that was it. a plane crash. those were the only guidelines we had received. and i wrote. and i rewrote. and i wrote. and i rewrote. my original idea was to have the people in my story crash on an island and to then start a war and kind of go all person versus person and create their own society (which i scrapped because that is impossible to write about. until i realized that was what lord of the flies was about...).

anyway, so i finally had an idea: everyone dies because of poisonous berries (hunger games in real life). i volunteered to go first because i really did not have a lot of confidence in myself in seventh grade and i just wanted to get it done because i hated public speaking. most people in my class were not really my friends and were not the group i ever hung out with (and most of them later turned out to be stoners but i really don't want to talk about THAT). and the teacher who was there was a young woman, she had come in the middle of the year to take the place of this male teacher who retired (he now teaches zumba on a cruise ship, man i wish i still knew him), and she was in the middle of grading papers. but i stepped up onto the podium and began reading and she stopped. and looked up. and i had her attention.

but when i finished telling the story and the ending was basically the characters in heaven, the class started clapping. and i looked over at my teacher and she literally wiped away a tear. and they were telling me so many nice things. the teacher said two things i have not been able to ever forget. "if i could i would publish that right now," and "i am not even going to read over it. i am just going to give you the A."

can you say confidence booster?

that summer was when i first made my poetry account. i was @nr_poems. all i wanted to do with that account was let people who suffered from depression know that they were not alone. i never really considered myself depressed but i had friends who were and when they would rant to me, i would write poetry as my way to produce a form of exhaling. but then a bunch of stuff happened with school and that account and blah blah blah i ended up deleting my account.

but then i missed writing so much i decided to make another account and now i am @nr.poems. and i am now happy. and i love writing. and i love reading. and there does not go a day where i do not think about writing.

and at one point in my life, i did not want to ever write again. i just felt depressed every single time i began to type. but in due time i realized how much it was truly helping me. my writing became the most important aspect of me. and there are so many people i want to thank. and there are so many amazing people i met as a result of these accounts, it is absolutely amazing. but i guess i will leave that for the end.

okay back to my introduction:

when i write, my name is not noah roselli, i am not a in high school, i am not however old i am, i am not even male. when i write, i am everything and nothing. i create these characters in my head and those are the people who are telling their story.

needless to say, some of the pieces in here are the most personal things that i have ever written.

wow i just rambled on for three pages.

okay okay okay.

i hope you enjoy my writing and you can find relation within these words, within these passages, these stories, these lives, and these characters. i hope you find meaning with every single thought, word, action, and stroke of the keyboard. i hope you find truth where there lies no veracity, light where there is only darkness, and perhaps darkness where there is only light.

but all in all i hope you enjoy.

thank you for taking the time to read this book, to read my mind.

here is where we begin:

noah roselli
nr.poems

*to everyone warned
about the fires but not
the firestarters*

table of contents

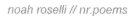

part one;

your eyes and other examples of black holes.
your heart and other examples of underwater chasms.

it is who we are

your eyes are black holes,
your heart is stardust,
and your mind is a nebula
waiting to combust.
your hands are dark matter,
your mind a shooting star,
and if you don't know what to do,
know this is who you are.

opposites attract

she always loved looking at flowers
while i was too busy with the starry sky.
she picked weeds clouded up in my brain,
but i saw the constellations in her eyes.

or opposites fall apart

and maybe i am a black hole
and you are a star
and that is why we never work out
in all the beautiful ways
that we want to.

not for me

she is a city of lights
and i am only one socket,
she wants to be in outer space
but i am a rundown rocket.

i fear heights

i built our love up into monumental heights
and i traced and carved out our names
into a plethora of million tiny stars in the nighttime sky
just so i could see a hint of your beautiful smile
stretch slowly yet strongly across your face
making me feel like i was falling
from the monumental heights
and dancing with the stars i used to call mine.

y=x sin x

we are traveling on two different wavelengths,
walking on different sides of this solid line;
we are living in two separate lonesome places,
looking for each other at two different times.

we are in two utterly opposite dimensions,
lost in translation and losing all of our strength;
we are translucent forms of opaque beings,
traveling on two different wavelengths.

i think i am drowning

i am treading between two oceans
drowning in all of my regrets;
i seem to move in slow motion,
i have been running out of breath.
my body is now one with the current,
i am not tossed by the waves anymore;
my body is cold but my heart is burnt,
i have gone too far to see the shore.
unfamiliarity is in this dark blue,
i am anxious in the space that is open;
looking for myself i have been losing you
i am treading between two oceans.

i do not know how long i can hold my breath

we are at the crest of civilization
and the trough of all existence;
sinking ships on choppy water
that will never go the distance.

we are broken and rundown
bridges without flowing water;
and the depths of the calloused sea:
majestic, but yet to be discovered.

and we never seem to take off
rockets without fuel will not go far;
losing balance on this tightrope,
this is all we will be, this is all we are.

vega

her soul was not made of stardust,
her soul was a true star; no wonder
she lit up every single room when she
walked into one. she was
the rarest form of a human being.
and i was so grateful to know her.

this is not about love

it was my period of obsolete disdain speckled with fits of sorrow and rage, an utter disgrace except upon the soul of a crestfallen (could you even say) human, all caused by a pinpoint in the carpet of time, the vacuum of space: the day of disembark when your touch faded from my hand and the earth turned, gravity functioned, and the sun rose without you present. how much sorrow seemed to take control of my soul: my skin begged for you, my nose pierced aromas and searched for the scent of you and only you. i try to find you in the stars in the nighttime sky and i call out your name but the only sense of welcoming is the silence consuming me in the darkness.

stars are only visible in darkness

and just like there is no darkness
without any form of light;
and there is no such thing as good
without something evil;
i do not think there is love
without first feeling
some emptiness.

this gravity did not hurt

it is like i was alone,
barely stumbling through outer space.
but your gravity pulled me in
and i think i finally know my place.

wonderland

you were my bermuda triangle.
but instead of losing ships,
when i was with you
i just lost my
mind.

ethereal

you were andromeda
and i was the galaxy of the eyes;
we were on different pathways
that would never collide.
funny how we grew weeds
with all the tears we cried;
there was no drought
but all of our flowers died.

we ~~are~~ were beautiful

i do not fully understand what is going on right now
but it is much of a fleeting feeling. as if when you love me
it is the minute past midnight on new year's eve
and the party which was once blaring is now suddenly
turning dim again and truly it hurts.
because at one point i know your love for me
burned brighter than a million stars.
but now it is just dead and vacant light
waiting to implode.

there is no oxygen in outer space: part i

i need you more than you could ever know and, sure, there will always be people ahead of me in your life; but know that i made you part of the oxygen i breathe and sometimes i need you when i feel like my lungs are going to collapse. so, it gives you no right to plant flowers in parts of me that are not open to the sun or to the air or to water because i have learned there is no point holding on to something so elusive when death is playing with your hair.
i made you my oxygen.
and i am stupid.
because you are gone.
and i cannot breathe.

there is no oxygen in outer space: part ii

these roots that clog my brain were planted by your calloused hands
but now you are somewhere in outer space and no one knows when
you will land.
in this darkness i will never see the light in your beautiful face,
though try as i might, i must remember: no one can hear you scream
in outer space.

the cliches in the color of the universe and you

we were sitting on the top of some hill in the middle of absolutely
nowhere when she looked at me, her silhouette contoured with the
outline of the stars making countless shapes in the clear sky
overhead, and said, "what color even is the universe?"
and countless visions of images taken by NASA flashed through my
head, showing every single color imaginable. "well honestly i do not
know, i just know for sure the universe is the same color as your
soul: color*ful.* from all of the places of darkness that counteracts with
all the wonderful spots of light, i know for sure that you are a soul
that i want to explore, much like the universe. you have a red chest,
with a heart of pure gold, and there are stars in the universe that
follow that color scheme. the nebulas that cloud the nighttime skies
are chalk full of purple, red and blue; and your body is a wonderland
with purple purity and blue misbeliefs. your soul is full of creations i
long to examine; the universe, to me, is the same. i don't know the
color of the universe, i don't know the color of your soul, all i know
is i want to discover both."

outer space

i wish i had realized
all of this sooner:
i wanted to land
among the stars,
but now i am
standing on jupiter.

the point of no return

when you go diving, there is one point where you begin to run out of oxygen, where you are already halfway to where you want to go to. and every single diver conjures the same question: "do i keep going? or should i swim back?" anywhere after that one place is past the point of no return, meaning that once you pass this invisible point, there is absolutely no going back, for you are already halfway done with your oxygen supply. everyone must decide if they should keep going; they have to decide if this point is the end of their journey, or the middle of it.

perhaps that is why people get attached to all the wrong things: they pass the point of no return.

perhaps, too, this is why i was so addicted to you. i was running out of air to breathe and i had gone too far beyond the point of no return, i succumbed to relying on you and i needed you to survive.

and trust me, this point of no return is one place i went with you.

you die twice: part i

if the sun were ever to burn out, eight minutes would pass before we knew it was gone; this is because light takes that long to travel from the sun to the earth. there are other examples of one million other distant places—stars, nebulas, and planets alike—that are about one hundred or one thousand light years away.
this means that when they die, we would not know for a long, long time.
this is the same with humans. when people leave, be it death or just leaving like all humans do, their light stays for a while, they are not truly gone.
so, like the saying goes:
you die twice. once when you actually die
and again when someone says your name for the last time.

when you bake, you should turn the pan halfway through baking time or it will bake unevenly. but in love, people love unevenly. how can that be avoided?

the veins in our arms that lead down to our hands are different in every single person, and, just like fingerprints, no two vein structures are the same. the common goal, however, of veins in every single person, is to have blood circulate around the body. so no wonder why people love unevenly, no wonder why no two people love the same person the same amount. because there are people whose veins flow all the way from the top of their head to the absolute end of their toes; love, then, flows everywhere within them. alternatively, there are people whose veins get the poisonous love pumped around the bend of their hips and to the edges of their fingers, but not to the tips of their toes. some people get too much love coursed through their body, while other people get just enough, or not enough at all.

but you coursed through my veins, you made me stay alive. and all i did to you was intoxicate you and give you the high you wanted but did not need. you said it was like being in an ocean with thalassophobia: you wanted love, but you feared not getting enough of it.

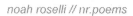

part two;

everything i will never waste precious oxygen, but wish i had the nerves, to say dear ex best friend

I.   i am truly sorry we ended on the terms that we did. if i could turn back time and stop our fight from ever starting, know that i would.

II. what we had was beautiful and there is no denying that. you were someone i was lucky enough to have in my life. and i hope you found yourself lucky when you were with me.

III. i am sorry for all the times that i yelled at you, all those times your trust in me slimmed down to a mere nothing. and i won't make up some sorry excuse this time telling you that i was doing this or doing that, because i know you take no crap.

IV. you taught me all that i know today. and i might say i regret it, regret being with you, regret the last decade of my life, but i do not. it was a memory i will cherish for many years to come. so thank you for being wise beyond your years. thank you for being the crazy person you were. thank you for making me have nights when i would go home and smile at my ceiling.

V.   i am sorry if i never showed you just how much i loved you but i never really had to. in all that i did, i did out of my love for you. i would comfort you when you needed comfort, i baked cookies with you, i played stupid games with you just to see you laugh or smile.

VI. those nights when we talked on the phone until the late hours of the morning are unforgettable. and thank you for calling me every single time i was about to go into the shower. and then laughing at me when i picked up the phone.

VII. i am glad we found ways to rekindle ourselves when our fire went out, but i am sorry i proceeded to burn everything down.

VIII. you introduced me to new songs, new television shows, new movies, new plays, new artists and new ways to be a better person. you told me when i was wrong and you helped me become right, thank you.

IX. you supported me for everything. and i could not ask for a person i would rather have had beside me.

X. thank you for all your advice, thank you for giving me a shoulder to cry on. i may say i do not miss some things, but i do miss you.

dear my best friend's future lovers

I.   when you tell her you love her, please mean it. do not tell her things you whisper to the back of every person's head with a heart brave and willing enough to break.

II. when she loves, she puts her entire body into it, she never feels only skin deep, she does not obsess over the idea of love, she feels it in her fingernails, her toes, the back of her thighs, and the tip of her ears. so when you love her, make sure it hits all critical veins, make sure you are infected, not just suffering similar symptoms.

III. when she is crying, kiss her tears and wish away the pain. when she talks, do not just hear, listen. when she hugs you, wait for her to let go.

IV. she has had her heart broken too many times by people who are worthless. do not make her look back on these months together and regret anything.

V.   when she smiles, cherish those moments, when she laughs, it means even more, because her mind is like a treasure map and you never know what you are about to explore.

VI. when she is gone, miss her like she is oxygen and you are drowning. and show her just how much she means to you. especially when she says she may never come back.

VII. when you touch her neck, make sure your hands are open, she has been stabbed in the back an insurmountable amount of times before. even if she loves you, her eyes will be wide open in wonderment making sure you do not hurt her. she used to be hurt by the people closest to her. now she is careful. let herself open up to you. she rarely does it. let her gain your trust. please.

VIII. she is broken and she has been far too damaged. do not be the reason for any more unnecessary but inevitable pain.

IX. treat her like a gem, not material.

X.   and do not, not even for the briefest of seconds, believe that she is replaceable. she is a love you will feel rarely. take it all in. and enjoy it.

dear everyone who has ever believed in me

I.   a life without you is not much of a life at all; who will be there at my worst, who will catch me when i fall?

II. i would rather live a thousand lives than live a day without you; you were there when i was yellow but stayed when i was blue.

III. we will float through galaxies and sail past millions of stars; you opened up all of my windows and helped unlock all my doors.

IV. life sometimes is a little crazy, life is sometimes a little tough, but you were always there to hold me even when it was rough.

V.   it is hard to live and not just exist, but i feel alive in the moment when you talk to me and tell me that i am missed.

VI. no one can ever drag us down, dragons will be easy to slay; because i know you will be there with a sword day after day.

VII. thank you for showing me just how much i was worth; i may have felt like fragile glass but you made me gold on earth.

VIII. this ship is sailing on choppy water, but i know we will never sink; because we are sturdier than we imagined, we are stronger than we think.

IX. you gave my life an entirely new meaning, i was holding my breath but finally i have moved on to breathing.

X.   thank you for supporting me, even when i walked on a fragile line; our love will move mountains and stand the test of time.

dear younger me

I.   it is okay to feel emotions that may overpower you, but do not let them be the downfall of relationships you are lucky enough to have.

II.   what you are going through may feel like the end of the world and you may cry yourself to sleep some nights, but it never is the end of the world. no matter what you think. things get worse before they can get better and it sucks, but it is the truth.

III.   humans are selfish. or people are selfless. there is sadly no in between. you may think you are balanced in this area of your life, but you will be always tilting one way or another.

IV.   but also know that there is a fine line between being selfish and being inconsiderate entirely of all other people's feelings.

V.   and know that there is also a fine line between being selfless and being fake. it is a fragile line. whenever you feel like you are walking on it, make sure you are thinking about other people.

VI.   when someone says they love you, do not jump on and say it back. people throw love around like it means nothing, but when you say it, you are supposed to mean it. so make sure you mean it.

VII. do not sit in the corner charging your phone at a party. get up and dance. even if you think you cannot. just do it. it will not hurt by trying. jump up and down and step back and forth, back and forth. do not be a wallflower. what will you be able to tell your children when they ask what your teenage years were like?

VIII.   you should be careful with who you give your blessings to. people take them freely and act like it means nothing.

IX. do not take anyone in your life for granted. everything is based off perspective: you may mean nothing to one person, but you should not beat yourself up because of that, for you will always mean the world to someone else.

X.   smile often and smile hard. read good books. watch multiple movies a week. when someone is talking to you, look them in the eyes. when someone is having a bad day, make sure you are there for them. when you hug someone, hug them with your entire body and let them let go first. crack stupid jokes, laugh loudly, and make other people smile. you never know who needs one.

dear my children

I.   you may think that i can never help you with what is
     happening in your life but i know what it is like to feel
     what you feel. everything you are feeling now, i have
     felt before. do not be scared to come and talk to me.
II. people play hard to get. it may not be you. maybe they do
     not want to be loved right now. do not run after
     someone who does not want to be chased. because
     some people run to be chased for fun, others run to
     hide. neither is good. do not waste your breath on
     someone who does that.
III. if you do not feel safe looking forward at your future, if you
     cannot stand to look behind you at the horrid past, you
     can look beside yourself and see me here. i will always
     be here for you even when you do not want me with
     you.
IV. be nice to everyone you meet, even if they are rude to you.
     always be the bigger person in a situation: you can
     forgive someone, but you do not have to let them back
     into your life.
V.   you are not defined by numbers.

VI. tears are not worth shedding if they are for someone who once meant the world and now means nothing.

VII. you will lose friends sometimes without a reason. do not dwell on the fact that they left. when life gets hard you will find your true friends. once one person in your life goes away, another will enter. it is just what happens to the equation of life. what you do on one side has to happen on the other: subtract one, add one.

VIII. do not go behind my back and do something you should not do. you can always come to me. i will bring you into a movie that is not approved for children, i will bring you to a party, even if people are drinking. because i will let you do anything as long as you show me that you can make the right choices.

IX. create nights you will remember, not ones that you will forget; in other words, it is better to go to a bookstore and get a cup of coffee with a few friends and have debates rather than go to a party you will barely remember the next day. create actual, real life memories. these are years you will only live once in a lifetime.

X. it is okay if you feel broken, but do not cut everyone around you on your pieces. you can ask for help with picking them up, but do not cut everyone.

dear anyone who will ever love me

I. my door is usually closed. my room is almost always a mess. my hair is sometimes placed under a hat. and even though i am flawed, i will love you like no one else has loved you before.

II. i may not always tell you when i am not doing okay. sometimes i will be crying and i will not tell you what is wrong immediately. but when i open my door and let you in, please, please, just be there to hug me. that is all i need. when my pieces are broken, put them back together.

III. i may not always tell you that i love you. just look for signs in all of my gestures. i will be here when you need me. we can play videogames together. we can read books and take turns reading aloud every chapter. we can go for long car rides. anything. my love is too powerful to let it go to waste on stupid things like me never saying i love you.

IV. i am bad at texting back. i am sometimes never on my phone. but when we are together in person, the last thing you will be is bored.

V. i might not be able to recall things about you. like what your favorite color is. or what your favorite movie, television show, book, or place to sit in your living room is. i probably won't even be able to recall what color your room is. but i will remember things like your smile or your laugh and with them i will recreate you in a series of words strung together so flawlessly it will be like looking into a mirror.

VI. fair warning: i might laugh at all the worst times. i might crack stupid jokes when i am happy. i might cry at the slightest of things. i may feel like i am moving on water that is making me sick all while standing on land. it is just who i am.

VII. i am sorry if i will hurt you. i am sorry if i become the reason for your tears or your heartache or the reason why you are having trouble. i will never mean for any of that to happen.

VIII. when you call me, i may not answer the first two times. and i may call back twenty minutes later with some lame excuse as to why i did not answer. but even when i say i don't care, i care. even when i don't show it.

IX. do not be afraid to kiss me at all the wrong moments because your lips are going to become my new favorite color and i am most likely going to be wondering what color will be created when ours mix.

X. when i say i love you, i mean it more than anything i have ever said before.

dear anyone who loves me

I. you are all of the traces of sunshine behind all of the
pouring rain, and you are the dopamine running up and
through my brain.

II. you are the cannonballs echoing through my head, you are
everything that is better left unsaid.

III. you are the lightning strikes going off in the dead of night,
you are all of the color in the monotonous white.

IV. you are the opposite of dreadful blithe, and you are the cure
to my calamitous life.

V. you are the music coursing in a silent room, and you are all
of the flowers when they begin to bloom.

VI. through the rain and wind, it is you that makes me a sturdy
boat; you are the only person i ever let cross over my
moat.

VII. you are the holster that holds my gun, i am the earth and
you are my sun.

VIII. even though i have a fear of airplanes you helped me in
flight, and even though i fear darkness, you are my
favorite type of night.

IX. you are the ravage that will neither hurt nor destroy, and
you are the reason for all of my love and all of my joy.

X. you are the chill running down my spine, and you are the
only thing i want to call mine.

dear anyone who has loved me

I. it has probably been a long time since we have last talked, and just know that even though i am smiling and even though i am laughing, even though i am far from wishing you were still with me, you still cross my mind.

II. i know that i say i am okay but the other day i was driving and i passed your street and i actually slammed my foot on the brakes as i began to think of you and all of our memories and i put my turn signal on but stopped myself from going and a row of cars began to form behind me and they all beeped in a desperate attempt to tell me to go but i did not go. i can never go.

III. i hope sometimes you think of me still. i still have nights when i just sit smiling about all of our happy moments together. i will never forget the time you put your head on my shoulder during gym class and i sat and braided your hair and you almost fell asleep and by the time i stopped you opened your eyes and asked me why i stopped and to start again and i do not know why i remember it but i do. even though that probably means nothing to you, it means more to me than you will probably ever know.

IV. it is truly sad to think that you meant the world and more to me but now, and never in a million years, will we ever again feel the same way about each other. it also hurts me that you once were my oxygen and i made you into the only thing that i would take the time to breathe in and breathe out but i was so stupid because you left me and now i can't breathe.

V. i like that we still talk. i used to think it would be hard to look at you or talk to you because we used to be in love, but it has been nice to actually hear you and not feel about a hundred different emotions eating at me. it was nice when you texted me and asked me some serious questions about my life, about how i have been. it's funny how we never dated but we still treat each other like we are broken up.

VI. i do not even remember having a fallout with you where we ended in a screaming fight and you stomped out and made the door crash with a loud bang at three in the morning. i think our fallout was more of a stop-replying-to-texts and stop-caring-about-how-the- other-person-was-doing and it is truly sad that it had to happen in that way because i know we could have been beautiful.

VII. i was asked the other day if i regretted any of my life decisions. i was asked if i could turn back time and change anything in my past, any of my worst life decisions, what would i change? i almost said you. but i didn't. because you were probably one of my best decisions and you were the reason for my pure happiness, the reason why i felt something stab me in the stomach but it ended up becoming one of the things where you became the reason for my pure despair and where i realized the pinch in my stomach was a tear in my heart.

VIII. i always feel this long desire to text you or call you or talk to you when you pass me by, to just call out your name and have a moment when we run into each other's arms and we collapse under our weight like in the movies. but this is life. not a movie.

IX. even though i do not act like it, i fucking miss you and i wish things were the same.

X. but at the same time, i never want you back in my life.

noah roselli // nr.poems

part three;

i seem to put out all the fires i start

warning label

i will treat you like you are royal
but our relationship will never be a monarchy;
i won't be a king, i will be a tyrant
and the only person you will worship is me.

i will yell about being burned
from every single fire i seem to start;
i am going to shatter all of your pieces,
walk away and then call you art.

i am the side effects to all medications,
the big crunch: the end of all the earth's creation.
i will take all that you have ever known
and twist it into a form of aberration.

i will make the smile that went from ear to ear
slim down like the moon until it is gone without a trace,
i will be the parachute that never opens,
the turbulence that begins without telling you to brace.

i do not have any matches, you are not friction,
but darling please be warned:
even though we are labeled as "fireproof"
we are bound to end up burned.

i will intoxicate you with my poisonous venom,
and have you square underneath my thumb;
i will turn all your joys to pain,
and hold your hand so hard it goes numb.

i will scream at all the little things,
stab you in the back until you bleed all over the floor,
forcefully make you clean up the mess
and pretend everything is the way it was before.

i will drive you to the point of insanity,
until you are cursing and screaming my name.
but when we reflect at the end of the day,
you will hurt, but i will laugh: "it's just a game."

you won't be able to say anything you want,
i will make you bite your tongue until you bleed.
i will be the destruction that renders you unconscious,
but make you think i am everything you need.

i will make your hair go from neat to messy,
mess with you until your eyes' sparkle begins to go dim,
i will turn from a drizzle to a hurricane
and people will point and say, "this storm is named after him."

your new smile will instead be a frown,
i will dress you up but give you a lead crown;
bring you into all of the oceans i created,
but hold you under until you drown.

i will take a razor and shear all the skin from your body,
then make you a skeleton in my closet.
i don't know what there is between us, but it is far from electricity,
all i will ever be is a burned-out socket.

i will give you a paper cut
turn around and ask you why you are crying,
i will stab you in the chest
and be distraught that you are dying.

i have a heart that's not ice, but coal,
don't come too close, your fragile bones might soften.
i will be the destroyer of all your white blood cells,
the delicate yet indestructible toxin.

i am the opposite of calm,
the definition of all that is chaos,
i am going to run away from you,
make you chase me down until we are lost.

i am going to find a way to pull every string you have,
until you become my personal marionette.
i am going to be the reason all your feelings converge
but give you amnesia each time so you forget.

i will tell you not to put your seatbelt on,
then purposefully drive off of our only road;
i am the silence before a bomb,
yet the only thing left standing after it explodes.

i am the bluest of the most heavenly skies,
yet the sound of lightning and the view of thunder;
i am the riptides and all of the currents,
yet still the only thing that is keeping you from going under.

i am not the angel of light but the monster that rose from hell,
the downfall of all that you have ever known;
i am the inexorable happiness but the inevitable sadness,
you know i'm bad for you but you never go.

there is no such thing as alice,
but darling i will always be your mad hatter;
i have some glue but that will not mean a thing
because i am the reason your ceramic glass heart will shatter.

i will satisfy all of your wildest dreams
but bring alive your fears from every nightmare,
i will break you away piece by piece
and be the one sitting there in deep despair.

i will never be your bright yellow sun,
but the dark grey rain;
i will never be the reason for your joy,
but instead all of your pain.

i am not the earth, the moon, or the sun
but you will fall into my gravitational pull.
i will take your sharpest points
and make sure they all go dull.

i will be the lightbulb that goes out,
the one that leaves you afraid in the dark.
i am going to be the lighter without fluid,
the one that never lights but burns some sparks.

but, see, all i am is a curse,
never your blessing in disguise
because all i will do is hurt you
and be the reason for your demise.

you will fall in love with my mind,
but never the true version of me.
because there is more to me that meets the eye,
there is more to read than to see.

i will say that you are okay
when you are at the furthest point from being stable;
you may be too tired to read my fine print,
so consider this my warning label.

i do not understand the world

i guess i do not understand the world
and frankly i have no idea why:
how is it that everyday someone saves
just to watch countless other people die?

and people try to ignore the fighting
and make love out of words like hate;
but why is it that the greatness of the world
is but a mediocre form of great?

i guess i do not understand the world
i do not understand the thieves or crime;
and people want to make a difference--
when is it better but in this time?

and there are certain people in this world
who find joy out of all the worst pleasures;
how can people think they have the power
to create trash out of others' treasure?

i guess i do not understand the world
nor all the hate, nor all the destruction;
why is it that people think they are allowed
to do things without any repercussion?

and people say it is a time to change
but no one seems to be standing up;
if we continue destroying the world
when will we be able to clean it up?

i guess i do not understand the world
i do not get the struggle or the fight;
how can someone look normal by the day
but be a killer by the start of night?

and we may suffer the consequences
of other people's unthoughtful mistakes;
but that does not mean we just brush it off
and act like it is something we can take.

i guess i do not understand this world
i cannot comprehend mistrust and hate;
we were a gold world but began to rust
but our destruction is not our fate.

it is not a matter of changing ourselves
for people will still live while others die;
instead, we must do what humans do best:
stand together to end this crime.

i guess i do not understand this world
for it is not a warzone, it is our home;
we need to look at all of these deaths
as people who died, not just a pile of bone.

for they were someone's brother or sister,
they were a friend and favorite teacher;
by committing these acts on innocent people
we are the lowest of all the creatures.

i guess i do not understand the world
and i may never fully understand;
maybe one day we will put the guns down
and instead walk the way humans should:

hand in hand.

wendy in wonderland

you wanted to go to neverland,
but we only went to wonderland
and try as you may,
you may never fully understand:

i never wanted to love you
but drive you as mad as crazy could be,
just take your lovely heart and shatter it in two,
then make you say you are crazy for me.

because there is no such thing as alice
and the queen of hearts will always survive;
i will love you and try to take your breath away,
because you may be breathing but you aren't alive.

your mind is the opposite of being weak,
strength and hardship, you will always endure,
i will take you apart piece by beautiful piece:
this is one thing i can promise you and ensure.

we will see grinning cats behind deviled eyes;
screaming "we are all a little mad here"
and bunny rabbits constructing crazed confusion;
asking profusely "would you like more tea, dear?"

upside down walls decorated beautifully
in rooms with no ceilings or floors,
i am going to shatter all of your windows
and unlock all closed doors.

black coats draped around our shoulders,
ghostly figures holding our hands.
we are trying to stay afloat sailing on choppy water
but we are sinking into the sand.

you cannot get lost if you have no destination
so, tell me how i got lost in your eyes;
i could destroy you for being so damn beautiful,
for being the reason for my demise.

my dear, alice did not fall down the hole,
i kicked her down after i kissed her cheek;
i will bring you down with me,
do not move, i know how to make you weak.

put your finger over my calloused lips,
do not dare to touch my heart,
if going away means forgetting,
i guess we fell apart at the start.

because you are not wendy, darling,
and i will never be peter pan,
you want to go all the way to the third star
but our first stop is here in wonderland.

i am not a human being

funny how my eyes are wide open
but i am far from ever seeing;
walking in line with my head held down:
i am not a human being.

funny how my chest is moving
but this air, i am not even breathing;
inhaling pain, exhaling joy:
i am not a human being.

funny how i am not asleep
but lost forevermore in endless dreaming;
burrowing fiction inside my soul
i am not a human being.

funny how i say these things,
empty promises that lost all meaning;
my "i love you"s are basic exhales:
i am not a human being.

funny how no one can hear me
while i sit here screaming;
wasting oxygen on uninhabited words:
i am not a human being.

funny how everyone is nodding their heads
when it is obvious they are disagreeing;
they do not like one word of what i am saying:
i am not a human being.

funny how my warm body
holds a heart that is close to freezing;
come too near and feel the chill:
i am not a human being.

funny how i am cut up my body
but not a part is bleeding;
empty veins, hollowed chest:
i am not a human being.

funny how i hurt your lovely mind
but you stay beyond your better reason;
you will die because of all of my mistakes:
i am not a human being.

funny how i hold you down
while these chains were made for freeing,
tired mistakes again and again:
i am not a human being.

beyond these lies you see the truth,
you say i am truly living.
but within the truth these lies are hidden:
i am not a human being.

oh, if only you knew

and oh, if only you knew,
i am not ethereal but a monster from hell,
i am the unbecoming of you,
the thing that makes you unwell.

but i am such a monstrosity
and you are blinded by my serene facade,
i am not a drizzle, i am a fucking hurricane,
broken, damaged, and flawed.

but i am an excrescence
and you do not even care about me,
i hate myself for hurting you,
but this is all i will ever seem to be.

and i am an abortion,
but you look past my evil qualities,
i am not a breeze, i am a monsoon,
bruised, hurting, and diseased.

you do not even see my damaged side,
you haven't got a clue,
i am hurting and i will hurt you,
but oh, if only you knew.

destruction

i guess there is destruction constructed inside of every strand of dna,
hamartia in each of my forty-six chromosomes;
a ravished stomach full of anguish and loads of disarray,
these four walls do not make up anything close to a home.

i think there is destruction masked behind my calm demeanor,
damage underlying every one of my sturdy bones;
it seems like lightning and thunder have begun to concur,
and i sit with a heart that is made up of nothing but stone.

i assume there is destruction running through all of my veins,
emptiness echoing throughout my hollowed chest;
there is nothing but desolation running up to my brain,
and causing conflicted pain is what i do best.

i suppose there is destruction mapped out in every heartbeat,
pain apparent in both of my blackened attempts of eyes;
melancholy, dejection, and my muse all taste so bittersweet,
and hatred has become the center of all of my lies.

i presume there is destruction on each of my many fingertips,
i stain and damage everything that i have ever caressed;
i have poison blotches on the top and bottom of my pink lips,
kiss me and become a part of this life, what a wonderful mess.

i understand there is destruction on the bottom of my feet,
and i walk on ice that is breaking underneath my every move;
i am always missing some piece of me, i am always incomplete,
my heart is not worth needing, it is not strong enough to ever
improve.

i believe there is destruction on my once tender, loving soul,
yet now, i live with a mind that is always under construction;
i have a burden that will never lift, a heart rendered inconsolable,
i guess all they say is true: i am the definition of destruction.

walking contradiction

you are a walking contradiction:
you like things smooth but you enjoy the friction;
you have brown eyes but you want blue,
you belong to many but you only love a few;
you said "no" while your head shook yes,
you like things clean but your room is a mess;
you were born in winter but you love the fall,
you thought you were a homerun but you were a foul ball;
you are a writer but all you do is trip over sounds,
you belong to the sky but are level on the ground;
you love real life but you dream in fiction,
you are a walking contradiction.

you are fire and i am water
and that is okay

you are a full-on monsoon.
and the water you have created is a place
most people seem to
drown in;

and i am a forest fire
with the ability to burn down
all the bridges i managed
to create.

you told me you were
invincible and fireproof
and i said i knew
how to dive and swim;

but you burned up and i burned out:
we fell in love
even though destruction
was our fate.

part four;

sometimes all love does is fail...

what the stars told me about you

i always thought that in my mind you would fade away. because perpahs in due time that is all the human mind is capable of: sparkly memories replace the dusty ones that cloud the shelves of our brains, constantly renewing who we are as a person.
but you, you were contrary to all of my beliefs. you turned into bubblegum that is now stuck on the bottom of my shoe.
you have been gone now for months on end.
i tried to keep track of how long it has been, but i lost count of the days after i hit twenty-one days, a solid three weeks, because i knew all the skin cells in my body had been replaced and your fingerprints no longer stained me. it should have been a sigh of relief over my entire body, a shiver in the hands of the breath from the god above, but it was the opposite of nostalgia. loving you was the opposite of nostalgia. loving you was hell.
instead of feeling okay, i felt like all my internal organs had been shifted and suddenly loving you was a sin. i felt your skin against my thighs, in my hair, and your kiss stained my lips like the coffee stain you left on my bed the day you told me you loved me in your boxers.
how can we go from cute mornings like that; thick black glasses and scruffy hair, omelet eating and standing in the kitchen in your boxers, kissing me and feeling the tug of unshaven hair against the delicacy of my cheek, warm and slowly bruising into a deep red; to an utter disgrace marked as a tragedy, but truly a blessing? how can we go from love poems and video games at three in the morning to not even making eye contact in the passing halls, not even a glance or a word muttered out of the corners of our mouths unless spoken behind turned backs?
it's funny. i used to wish on stars to find someone like you.
i would walk at night just to see stars, just to wish on that first star i saw, just to wish for you. and then we fell in love. and then we fell out of love. if all we do is get hurt when it comes to love, why the hell do we even bother?

when i fell in love with you, i warned you. i told you that i was a writer and that i do not remember key indulgences that other people tell me. i never open myself up enough to fully envelop who people are: i could not even tell you my best friend's favorite color or favorite movie, yet i opened myself up to you. i would forget things upon weeks of them happening but somehow i have the ability to recount our adventure of love, our eminent beginning and our suave destruction.

we fell in love on a saturday. at least i did. sitting in your basement with two of your douchey guy friends and one of my girlfriends, playing that stupid guess-the-word game, some half hour past the stroke of midnight, some might call it a friday night, i call it saturday morning, when i fell in love with you. it was mid-december, the dead of winter, when i caught that look in your eyes, that look that destroyed me. you were the medication to my disease and slowly i was becoming addicted to you.

you looked at me when i left that night and you smiled and it was such a rare sight to see that i treasured it when i went home that night, tucked it into the back of my pocket and replayed it until i fell asleep smiling and laughing into my pillow, until my mind was almost as happy as my heart.

so, we fell in love in the winter, when the snow was piling up outside your doors and all of our windows were shut so that the cool air wouldn't mess up our warm bodies against each other, the warm breath of the kisses we gave each other on our necks and shoulders. i do not know when you began to fall for me, but before the drops of white melted, we were one.

"i love you," you said within a few weeks.

"no, you do not," i said back.

"i love you," and i knew you meant it.

suddenly i found myself not wishing on those stars. suddenly i did not need anything else in my life. i found the only thing i needed when i was next to you. and i cannot thank you enough for giving me moments of happiness in my life which was black and white. you put color in my life when i needed it most and now my life has not changed from that beautiful bubbliness you left within me.

i still remember the stupidest things about you, but they give me something to look back and smile about, i guess.

the first time we walked into starbucks together and waited in that ridiculously long line just so you could have me try something you deemed as delicious, for example.

i stuck with my normal black iced tea, sweet. you got a warm caramel apple cider that you said filled your head with delirium, and when i took a sip it filled mine with something too but i think it was something more delirious because my lips touched where yours did seconds before and it was still stained with an aroma that made my head spin a little bit. or maybe it was your eyes and the way you smiled when you said my eyes lit up as i drank the cider, nodding in agreement with its deliciousness.

and then the second time we walked through the same doors, we both ordered warm apple cider, drinking it as our arms interlocked at the elbows, our breath clouding in front of us, freezing our asses off on the park bench, our throats warming up from the cider, our minds from our kisses.

i still order warm caramel apple cider.

i also remember how obsessed you were with astrology and would always screenshot those textposts about you being a taurus and i, a libra. we used to laugh for hours on end at the accuracy, or for that matter, the inaccuracy, of those stupid posts. i saw one the other day that you had showed me. comparing us to seasons not attributed to our own: i was summer, even though i was born in fall; and you were winter, even though you were born in spring. how accurate. i am sweet like summer is, you are cold, so bitterly cold.

and i remember our love as if it still echoes in my mind.

and i remember our love month by trivial month.

and i remember our love and i remember our love and i remember our love.

and i remember you

and i do not know if i am heartbroken or if i am thankful that you are not here anymore.

but all i know is you are gone and you are moving on and i should be too. and i took a walk the other day at night, and i looked up at the stars and they seemed to be laughing down at me. they seemed to be telling me how stupid i am for wishing for you, how stupid i am for loving you. but, i mean, i guess i saw a star somewhere within you. but you were a supernova and supernovas are the beginning of a star's death.

i always thought in my mind that you would fade away.

but you never did. and maybe you never will.

no smoking

she only loved me when my eyes were shots of the hardest liquor and my kisses were speckles of cigarette butts; those were the countless days and the infinite nights when she kissed me like she needed me to survive, like she needed me and my love for gravity to function and the world to revolve, even though there are three unstoppable forces: gravity, magnetic or nuclear forces and, of course, love. but her words still resonate deep within the confines of even the most cryptic parts of my aerodynamic mind, her words create something within me that moves the deepest parts of my soul even though the words she had muttered to me were that she was empty, her chest held a cage and inside that, nothing; her veins were flowing atoms of oxygen and nothing else; she said she was so empty that she does not know and maybe never will know what it means to be full, except when that fullness comes from the lean back swig of a shot of alcohol and the sweet sugar radiating off of the ends of burning paper; she was so empty, she filled herself up with drugs, and when she filled herself up with drugs, she filled herself up with the ugliest form of love: when love means cold and unmade bedsheets in a clump on the floor next to the bed, and the clothes that were on her body are thrown everywhere but into the drawers they came from. she was never okay, she was never full, never satisfied with the easiest satisfactions, unless she was high off of some substance. she was deteriorating all of her insides, kissing my lips, and calling that love. she is not love. we are not love. because she only loved me when she was drunk, only when the words echoing in her mind told her that if she did not say my name she would not be okay. she only loved me when she was high. but my heart is an area where smoking and drinking are not allowed.

art: i

you compared me to art the first day we met.
you started by calling me **Mona Lisa**.
there was some mystery behind my eyes, and according to you, there
was also some grand story behind my smile, just like **Da Vinci**'s
masterpiece.
you held out your hand and i took it within mine and shook it up and
down and you smiled as you said your name and it grew even more
when i said what mine was.
you worked in a museum, night shift, tonight was your first day off
in a while, so you came to your favorite place, of course a coffee
shop; it was perfect with the "jazzy live tunes, the atmosphere" and i
joked that "no, it is because you are trying to be a hipster" and you
laughed and said, "fine then you must be attempting to be a hipster as
well."
and i smiled and took a sip from my hot, well warm, i was too busy
talking to you, caramel coffee. and you asked me when i came here
for the first time and i said that i had been going to this place for two
years, ever since my friends introduced it to me as a new-wave slash
bar-for-the-coffee-drinker and they were undergoing their hipster
phase.
and as i was about to get up and leave after talking for a good hour,
about the music, about what it was like to work night shift in a
museum and if it was ever *Night At the Museum*ish, and again you
laughed, and i felt my stomach tighten and i felt my heart flutter, and
then drop within my stomach, you wrote your number on a napkin
with a black border around the outside, putting down your name in a
nice cursive lettering.
"give me a call" you said,
"**Mona Lisa**," you said.

art: ii

our second date, you called me a **Vermeer**.
you were always obsessed with **Vermeer**'s painting techniques: the
contrasting lights, the use of shadows and the way colors seemed to
meld together into one true uniformed picture.
we walked in the park at three o'clock in the afternoon, your hands
were in your jean pockets, your shoulders were pointed up, clearly
you were cold: you gave me your jacket and it draped around my
shoulders, too big and burly on me and your mouth created a cloud
of fog with each exhale of warmth contrasting the cold November
air.
it was picturesque. fairytale-esque.
the bare trees glistened with the same water that was collecting on
the ground.
we stopped into the coffee shop we met in to attempt to warm up our
frosty insides. the first sip i took of my hot coffee, i felt it travel
down inside of me.
you, on the other hand, ordered an iced macchiato, even though you
were basically frozen.
when i brought it up with you and asked why, you just shrugged, and
so we went back outside, you sipped from your straw as i sipped out
of the take-out mug.
at one point, you stopped walking.
when i noticed and asked if something was wrong, you brought your
finger up to your mouth and shushed me behind closed eyes. when
you opened them again, your eyes intense, you smiled and said, "i
am just trying to take all of you in. you are beautiful. and the way the
light hits you from this angle," you paused, you raised your hands
into nothing, "**Vermeer** wasted his time painting those other women,
he should have painted you."

art: iii

you said **Andy Warhol** was your favorite artist.
on our third date i asked "why?"
"he has a way with words," you replied.
I laughed "but he is an artist. he paints. how—"
"exactly. he is an artist. yet he invokes some feelings. his work
makes me want to say something, makes me want to change
something within myself. he creates something intangible yet so
close to grasp." he turned to me and smiled, "and now you are
looking at me like i have ten heads," you laughed, "i guess maybe i
am just tired, not making sense."
but i agreed silently. because you did not know but you were my
Andy Warhol.
and so we sat and ate breakfast together, even though you were
beyond exhausted, as you were beginning to tell me that you got into
the museum at nine and did not leave until a little after eight in the
morning, but you said that you would rather be with me then
sleeping.
and so we sat at that restaurant outside in the cold air, the sun gone
from the sky, and you ate your oatmeal and i ate my belgian waffle
and after each spoonful you would say something else to me, ask me
another question, reply to one of mine.
and suddenly a wave of something washed over you.
"i know why i love **Andy Warhol** so much." and my silence led you
to continue, "he was so lonely and that is one of the biggest reasons
for his art. i find something relatable in his art. i was lonely. and his
art was always there."
the last thing i said to you that morning: "you do not have to be
alone."

art: iv

Pablo Picasso, according to you, was brilliant.
on our fourth date, you took me all around the museum and every
single time we passed a **Picasso** you stopped walking, stood with
your hands on your hips and a smile on your face, took a deep breath
in and continued walking.
believe it or not, i was jealous of the art for having you look at it like
that.
i only wished you would look at me like you would at art.
and so i followed you around like a duck waddling behind its mother
and you held my hand, but were in front of me, leading me.
you were showing me a painting when a man came out of nowhere
wearing the same security jacket as you and he messed up your
already messed up hair and gave you a little pat on the back and
shoulders slash "bro-hug" type thing where one hand was on your
back and the other in your hand. and then he turned to me.
and you said, "meet joshua."
and i shook his hand and said with a smile, "pleased to meet you,
joshua."
and he smiled and shook his head back and forth, shaking my hand in
the process. "please," he said, "call me josh." he turned to you and
said, "is this the one that you have been telling me about lately?"
and you looked like you were about to kill him.
but all i wanted to do was take your head in my hands and kiss you
everywhere.
you are as beautiful as one of those **Picasso** paintings.

art: v

on our fifth date, you said the sky looked like a **Jackson Pollock**.
we sat on top of the hill that night, waiting for the sun to set while it
overlooked the vastness placed in front of us, because finally winter
was melting into the faintest forms of spring.
the sky seemed to disappear and disintegrate into itself, folding over
into an ombre of colors.
the reds and yellows of the sky disappeared and nighttime set in and
before i knew it the moon was hanging in the sky and stars were
speckled everywhere.
it definitely was **Jackson Pollick**ish, it seemed like God threw stars
in the sky like **Pollock** did to his canvas, random splashes of paint
here and there.
"it is breathtakingly beautiful," i said.
"it really is," you replied.
and then i turned to you. but you were already looking at me. i
smiled, and you smiled back, and for the first time i had noticed your
face was like one of his paintings, it was speckled with random
splashes of beautiful light brown freckles.
and so we were on the ground just sitting there for hours, finding
memorable and old constellations as i made new ones on your face.
when we were sitting there, you said your favorite piece of
Jackson's. it was one i have never heard of before: **The Deep**.
when i looked it up later, i think i fell in love with it too.
almost as fast as i was falling for you.

art: vi

Claude Monet's work was always done with delicate care, the colors
in each piece of work were light and airy, full of blues and yellows,
greenery and water.
on our sixth date, when it was finally warm enough for the first buds
of some types of flowers to finally appear, we took a nicer walk
through the park than the one we took on our second date.
the park was alive with the buzz of the talking of people and
waddling and quacking ducks.
and as we were walking you picked up some pebbles and held them
in your right hand while my right hand held your left hand. and we
found our way up onto a bridge, where the voices of people
disappeared, and the traffic congesting the roads of new york city
seemed to melt into a low buzz and instead, all we heard was the
steady stream of the water beneath our feet.
you leaned against the railing overlooking the water and you were
silent but somehow it was enough to just be next to you. "how
Claude Monet is this scene?" you barely exhaled.
you threw some pebbles down into the water and after a few minutes
you looked over at me.
after staring for a second, i laughed, "what?" i asked.
"nothing" you replied. "i just, i love you."
"no, you don't," i said back.
"no, i love you." you echoed.
and i know you meant it.
and we stood there, our torsos extending past the railing, but not
extending past our centers of gravity, yet the force i felt with you was
enough to make me fall.
i did not say it that day, but i love you, too.

art: vii

our seventh date was in the summertime: nice and hot. on another
night you had off, you invited me over to your apartment and cooked
a dinner and bought the finest wine you could afford.
"kiss me, Mona Lisa" you breathed as you came closer to me, our
bodies touching as you unbuttoned the first button on your shirt after
dinner was done.
and so i did just that, i touched my lips barely against your own.
"Mona Lisa, i want to have you," second button, third button.
but i did not want to have you.
"you are my disease and i never wanted to be cured," you said.
unbutton.
"you are so beautiful," unbutton, "hot," unbutton, "sexy," and your
shirt was off.
you pushed me down onto my knees and said, "Mona Lisa i want to
be with you."
but i said no. i said i am not ready. i said no, please no.
i said i do not want to. i said stop.
i pushed you off of me. well i tried to.
i breathed you in and you were poison in my veins and now i cannot
fucking breathe.
i said stop, i said stop, i said stop, i said stop, i said i do not want to, i
said stop, i said stop.
but you did not hear me. you never listened to me anyway.
our seventh date was in the summertime: nice and hot. but you were
so cold.
but how ironic. you compared me and the rest of our love story to art,
and you tell people not to touch the art,
but you put your hands on me.

art: after

after writing all of our dates down in the notebook i seem to always
carry under my arm while on the bus ride over, i see you for the first
time in five and a half months, sitting down in the same cafe we met
in, and you are alone, waiting for me, and i wonder why i decided to
meet you here.

but through swift glances from side to side, you manage to cast your
eyes onto me and you smile and stand up. i smile back and walk over
to you and we give each other one of those awkward hugs that we
always talked about hating, i guess that makes us both hypocrites;
but you call me Mona Lisa again and it sends memories down my
spine. then comes small talk:

"so how are you?" you ask with a sigh, sitting back until your spine
meets the chair.

"i have been good. i have a boyfriend now, he works in the firm on
the floor above me," i say back, knowing i should not, but glad that i
did, talk about him to you, "what about you?"

you move your shirt a little and lean back up towards me, "oh me? i
have been great. the museum is good and like you, i found someone
new, too."

a blonde bob-cut makes her way to our table and places down a
brown coffee in front of you and in front of me—"black hot tea," i
looked up and you were smiling at me, "you remembered?"

"how could i forget?"you reply.

sips of coffee, tea, and small talk later you talk again, "you know i
had planned how i was going to propose to you."

"really?" i ask, my insides warming up with the tea.

"yeah, and i know, i know, we were dating for like what twelve,
thirteen months?"

"almost fifteen, yes." sip.

"fifteen months. and i thought you were the one. but i wasn't going to
ask you soon, i was just planning on doing it."

"talk me through it." sip.

"i was going to wait until probably our two or three year anniversary, bring you here and relive the first night we met. i was going to get that band that was playing—what were they called? something weird like 'oranges' or some other dumb name. anyway, i was going to try to recreate that night and then i would tell you that i loved you. and boom. we would be married."

i chuckle, "what makes you think i'd say yes?" sip.

"would you have?"

"yes i would have."

your face became serious, the smile stretching down. "Mona Lisa, i am so sorry. i am sorry for hurting you and destroying you. i am sorry that night i made a big mistake and did things i should not have ever done to you. you do not have to forgive me but i have to know that you know how sorry i am. and if i could turn back time and slap myself in the face and say like 'man, do not be an idiot, you are going to hurt her' i so would have."

i smile, "i second that."

you laugh and i see your posture loosen and your spine misalign itself. you collapse into yourself like the black hole you are prone to become, the black hole that destroyed me. comfortability is different from excessive contentment.

i continue: "i don't know if i can ever forgive you. but let me just say this: you compared our love story to art. you said i was like art. but what is one thing that all artists, no matter what, do?" i saw you formulating, but you stopped looking me in the eyes, as if to show just how much more you were thinking, "they all make mistakes. Leonardo Da Vinci painted over the Mona Lisa three times. and i hope you do not take this as a way to forgive you, this is not acceptance: i am trying to say that that was art. but i am not art. you cannot paint over me when you mess up. you cannot change me. you cannot. so i hope you know that i loved you." i paused.

"but goodbye."

the loves i had but never finished

and her name was lilac;
even though she hated purple and loved blue.
we had something that couldn't be traded for the world
ever since the day we were two.

but to her, my name was just white noise,
and she was having trouble within herself to concentrate.
so she turned me on and left me playing,
now i know she smiles but all i see are my mistakes.

and her name was francesca;
she lived in a town not far from my own.
and we used to talk into the late hours of the night
only staying up by the vibration of a phone.

but to her, my name was the inhale of a cigarette
and she had been longing for quite some time to get high.
so she breathed me in and then exhaled me out,
and before i knew it she left without even saying goodbye.

and her name was eliza
we met when we were only thirteen.
and we may have been young but we were in love
we were just two kids living in a dream.

but to her, my name was pouring rain
and she had just been in a two and a half year drought.
she took me in and then began to let me go,
because she was a riddle i had never truly figured out.

and her name was michelle
she said she loved me the first day we talked.
and we said we would never let each other go,
she held my hand whenever we walked.

but to her, my name was lively
and she had been living for years in dreadful monotony.
and even though she let go of me,
she left me seeing some things i have never before seen.

and her name was antonia
she loved many before she loved me,
i always thought she would be the girl
i would question on one knee.

but to her my name was delightful
and she never had someone she could talk to as intensely.
she used me, tied me up in chains,
but dressed me in a facade that made me feel like i was free.

i don't know why i loved all of these girls,
why i let them impact my world.
because they all left without me,
opened me and left me unfurled.

but there are some things i regret,
and loving them has never been one.
they may have left me stranded,
but they made me the man i have become.

love war

i can hear the cacophonous bugle melody,
and on my nose is stained the metallic scent of blood;
what a shame this war has now been lost----
you and I, the two casualties in this war on love.

flowers in my lungs, flowers in my head

you breathed life into me
it filled my lungs
and coursed through
all of my empty veins.
but there is no light,
nor is there oxygen in my brain:
they will die, they will die
until nothing remains.

first come, first served

she loves
like there are
no ends to the earth;
so her heart
is always the one
to shatter first.

history museum

she belonged in a museum
but for all the wrong reasons;
she was not art, she was history
and my heart knew the reason.

opposite sides of the same edged sword

you were green when i was yellow
your name inside my mind
was the only thing that ever dared to echo.

i turned orange when you became blue
my past was completely forgotten
but all of my future belonged only to you.

but you are now infrared and i am ultraviolet
in this kingdom we promised a monarchy
but our kingdom has suddenly become your tyrant.

and now our rainbow is drained, our color is completely gone
in this chess game we were playing together i should have been
royalty
but instead all i was treated as was a little pawn.

beautiful

~~we are beautiful~~. *no, we are not.*
~~we are so beautiful~~. we *used to* be beautiful. we used to be absolutely and irrevocably beautiful. we were all of the colors in the rainbow and all of the shades of love in all of the tints of the unknown. we were the greatest thing that could be created out of living. we were inhaling each of our loves and exhaling all forms of beauty. we are so beautiful. we used to be exquisite forms of the best beings, we used to be the source of life for each other. we were air for each other and we were air for each other and we were beautiful and we were so beautiful.

but i learned in chemistry that carbon monoxide is made of two simple elements: one atom of carbon and one atom of isotopic oxygen. alone, both of these things are needed to live, but **together they are a deadly concoction**. and i mean maybe your heart was oxygen and my lips were carbon but all i know is ~~we are beautiful~~ we were beautiful and we fed off of each other for life. all i know is that we were inseparable but for all the wrong reasons. we were inseparable because we bonded together like atoms of carbon and oxygen and honestly, we coexisted as one and we thought we were beautiful, we thought we were *so goddamn* beautiful but we were **a deadly concoction of the ugliest atoms**. and we were not anywhere close to being beautiful we were the opposite of beautiful we were chaotic and we were killing each other. we are not beautiful we never have been anywhere except in the vacancy of beautiful. our love is terrible.

and honestly, we used to be the rainbow we used to be as beautiful as a rainbow and we used to be the rainbow but all of our colors have faded into the ugliest greys and all of the muted blacks and metallic whites screaming with the buzz of emptiness. we used to be beautiful we used to be so beautiful we used to be unmistakably beautiful.

~~we are beautiful~~. *we are not **beautiful** anymore.*

that is not love

venomous kisses mistaken for blisses and dismissed as well as forgotten. but teeth turn rotten even from something sweet like candy; and the underneath of my body ties knots into itself because it has not forgotten your opaque mistake which was mistaken for love, yet this love caused your "little snowflake" to break.

and that is not love.

and how can powerful be beautiful when powerful is you and you are not full of beauty? you have dulled the feelings of pain and pulled out my heart in the process, but i guess this ending was fate because you always told me how much you hated the shape of my body so you dictated that you needed to destroy me in order to please you. and i have debated leaving you but have waited because you sedated me to those longing feelings of pain.

and that is not love.

you have a tongue and a heart that may not be serrated but still cut they are sharp. and in the darkness that consumes me i feel as if i am free from what we were and i feel like what we are becoming is becoming undone. and honestly it would hurt much less if you were to come at me with a gun, because at least then you would shoot me and it would all be done, all of this love and pain will be gone.

and that is not love.

and a thousand kisses do not make up for the hundreds of bruises that you left on me and if only everyone around me could see my silent plea that i have introduced is masked by a facade of laughter and a brick wall of smiles.

and that is not love.

and while you go about your day i am a thousand miles away from who i was before i met you. and honestly you have committed murder in the third degree for causing this pain which you distorted for trying to make me feel supported on glass that is breaking. and if i could ask for any one thing, i would not ask for you, for i have been faking this love.

and that is not love.

and it is as if you ripped out the box that holds my voice but know that if i had a choice between life and death, one of them has the option of never again being with you. and i can scream, i can shout, but you never hear me, you never even seemed to listen to me and, frankly, i fear being with you; because, my dear,

our love is not love.

the definition of sad

i used to be fire, but lately i have felt myself becoming stone and i have grown insurmountably cold and i have told myself that the bones that i have known my whole life are the furthest thing from a home because i have felt myself lose hold of the happiness. i am losing my happiness. and i am giving in to the sadness because i have nothing left to give. and the pain of remembrance has become so overwhelming that i have nothing left to give. because at one point i was gold on the surface but after spending weeks out in the rain it would become certain that i would rust and give in to the pain and i am worthless and imperfect and worth less than threefold of a dime and in essence all i am is a semblance, resemblant to an empty mind, a beautiful emblem masking the most horrible venom, fading away in due time. and to others the pain may not seem like enough but it's enough to let me know that i do not want to live and it may seem crazy coming from a guy who tells other people to look to their future and to tomorrow even though he wouldn't mind not having a tomorrow and doesn't see a future for himself, one who wants to live but has nothing left to give. i try. i try so hard every single day, but every single day i try is another day i wish to die. and i cannot breathe. i am not breathing. i try to fill my lungs with air but my moving chest is deceiving. because i am partially incompetent, fully denominate. and even though i act so tough, my ego is like a monument, i am not even confident, i cannot take a compliment. and lately i have been feeling the opposite of opulent. the opposite of happiness. the opposite of glad. the opposite of okay. the definition of sad.

you say i destroyed you, but you destroyed me

we fell in love as if we had a clue that the same eyes that held an entire galaxy and poetry great beyond compare would be the same eyes that would cause us to break, that the same sad eyes that held love would be the same sad eyes that held destruction.

we fell in love as if we had a clue that the same lips we loved to kiss would be the same lips that had the ability to destroy an entire relationship, the same lips that held words of adornment would be the same lips that held words of departure, the same lips that whispered sweet nothings against our ears under white duvet covers built upon a bed of dreams would be the same lips that screamed everything but nothing, everything but dulcet words with connotations of positivity.

we fell in love as if we had a clue that the same hands we would hold until our knuckles turned purple, the ones that we would kiss the folds and grooves, the nails and the wrist, would be the same hands that would choke each of our necks until we were barely breathing, thinking that love was the reason our breath was being taken away, not realizing that we were choking on words that should have been better left unsaid, not realizing that the tickle at the back of our throat was the lack of oxygen caused by the other person's lack of love.

we fell in love as if the same heart that was spent laying on top of most of the time, listening to the steady bum bum—the beat that lets us know that each one of us is as alive as the other, that each of us is feeling the same intensity of love, the same head-over-heels feeling of being one hundred and fifteen percent crazed to capacity—would be the same heart that we would hear slowly begin to shatter, the same heart that we loved would be the same heart that would be destroyed with a few words, a few mindless words that came from the bottom of our stomachs, not the bottom of our hearts, the bottom of our empty stomachs, not the bottom of our hearts that beat for love, our hearts that used to beat for love, for, the hearts that were full of love are now the hearts that are full of anything but the latter.

we fell in love as if we had a clue that the same mind we loved to get
to know, the mind that we each fell in love with because of the other
things that each of us loved—anything from the cities we loved to
visit or the books that made us cry, from the movies that made us feel
like we would never die to the grocery list that we had memorized—
would be the same mind that we would never get to hear the thoughts
of again except for the final thoughts of a destructive relationship
that had the foundation equal to a prism trying to balance on its edge
and not on its face because we tried to be delicate but it never
worked because the minds that we fell in love with are a destructive
ticking time bomb, unaware of its true degree of destruction, yet its
ending was eminent; the same mind that we fell in love with would
be the same mind that told the heart to stop beating for love and the
lips to speak words that destroyed us and the hands to choke us and
the eyes to break us.

we fell in love as if we had a clue that we would fix each other just to
break ourselves even more. we fell in love as if we had a clue that
destruction was as predictable as the sun rising after it sets, as
inevitable as the oceans to form waves that come crashing into the
sand: we fell in love as if it was not obvious to see the inevitable.
we fell in love we were in love.
we were in love. we fell in love.
we fell in love. we fell in love.
only to fall apart, we fell in love.

but all good things fall apart.
you say i destroyed you
picked up your heart
then threw it away.
but how petty must you be
to stand up
and take my heart for yourself.

you say i destroyed you
but you turned my life into a living hell.

you say i destroyed you, but you destroyed me, too.

the mind reaper

i never thought that the vision of death
        could be found within the confines of human features;
        but i guess a scythe and a black headdress
        are what lies behind my lover's unblemished demeanor.

he hid in a facade of darkness in overpowering light,
        and he said he would love me until the day of my death;
        it was true, for he muttered those words on my last night,
        right before he stuck a knife in my back and i took my last
        breath.

i was the victim in a love murder from a serial killer,
        who was charged with nothing but misdemeanor;
        he has a warm hug, but his heart belongs inside the freezer:
        for, he is the heart, soul, dream, and the mind reaper.

part five;

...but sometimes love works;
it is the journey of finding out whether the love we feel is genuine or
not that leads the human heart and brain back to love, even if it is
destined to end.

the story of a girl

there once was a girl
whose heart was made of *gold,*
she said she fell in love
with all things uncontrolled.

there once was a girl
whose favorite color was ***black***,
she said she often put out
more than she ever got back.

there once was a girl
whose soul was *yellow* stardust,
she wore a caged heart
made with metal that would never rust.

there once was a girl
whose cheeks were a muted *red,*
"just because you know me
does not mean you love me," she said.

there once was a girl,
whose body was a joyous *orange* sunrise,
i fell in love with her soul
and the brightness in both of her eyes.

there once was a girl,
who said she lived in shades of *blue,*
sadness was her heaven
she was bruised and beaten, too.

there once was a girl
whose tongue danced in *red* delight,
how lovely she looked at me
oh, what a rather beautiful sight.

there once was a girl
whose hair was a perfect shade of *brown*
she kissed me like she was the ocean
and in it i would be the one to drown.

there once was a girl
who saw in shades of black and *grey*
i loved her with all of my heart,
to each other we would never betray.

there once was a girl,
whose lips were a kissable shade of *pink*
she put them on me one night,
while she leaned against the kitchen sink.

there once was a girl
whose eyes were the deepest *green*
she told me not to call her princess
because she wanted to be treated as a queen.

there once was a girl
whose heart was made of *gold*,
she had a soul that would never be bought,
it was too rare to be sold.

there once was a girl
you could say with whom i adore,
and maybe she loves me too—
i guess this is what our lives are made for.

until death, my love

they say you only get one miracle,
but everyday with you is a marvel sent from above;
from heart to heart, from chest to chest,
you and i, until the day that we die, my love.

my mind is not constrained by chains, my heart is still ablaze.
your eyes are friction, my body the match, no wonder i feel warm
disarray;
the fire that we have created is kindled with care:
te e me, fino al giorno che moriam, il mio amore.

they say you are in love when you can't picture a life without
someone
but i guess that makes you all of my future, all that i adore;
my past is not apparent when i am with you:
vous et moi, jusqu'au jour où nous mourrons, mon amour.

even if time is not on our side, destiny not written in our path,
know that this love is something i will never be able to forget;
thank you for your heart, for opening up my mind: i will forever
remember, it will be:
du og jeg, helt til den dagen vi dør, min kjærlighet.

to create heaven on earth is all we will ever try,
waking up next to you every morning is all i have thought of;
this love is all we have, this love is all that we will ever need:
you and i, until the day that we die, my love.

reassurance in love

"i believe in change," he muttered to me as he sat on my couch at three in the afternoon just after school had ended, "you know? i believe that this morning you woke up a different you than the you you were yesterday. and i believe that tomorrow you will be entirely different than you were today. i believe you change daily, that your cells die and reproduce and that there is a new set of cells in your body every single day. and maybe this is the reason that you and i are working out as long as we are and maybe that is the reason that love is such a wonderful thing: the you i fell in love with months ago is different than the you you are now. and that is amazing. people do not necessarily change as much as they grow. i am learning new things about you every single day and every single day i fall in love with you more. because tomorrow the fingers touching me will not be the fingers that are grabbing my hand right now," as he said this he brought his hand closer to his chest and he put both hands around my one hand, "and i love that about you and i love that about love and i love that so much. we are never going to be the same person ever again. just like how there are no two of the same fingerprints in the world or there are no two of the same snowflakes or no two worlds out there that are the same shape or size or have the same atmosphere, that should scare me," he looked into my eyes, "but it makes me love you more." and i leaned in closer to him as he continued, "i love you and i do not care how much i have to tell you this in order for you to fully grasp that i mean it. sure, i love using chopsticks, and i love music, and i love books that make me cry, and i love my family and my dog, but with you, there is a love on an entirely different level. and if you ever, i mean if you ever, feel that i am slipping away from you remember that i am exploring your mind. and your mind is a map and although i will definitely get lost a few times, trust me, the destination is well worth it."

supermarket lover

"i do not want us to end. i do not want us to ever have to end. i do not want to be in the supermarket one day and casually run into you and awkwardly say hi. i do not want to have to catch up on all things concerning your life and your love. and i do not want to make small talk about the weather and discuss the horrible economy. because you mean the world to me and i do not want us to end. i do not want us to end because you tell me all of your hopes and all of your dreams and the way you want to make an impact on the world at two in the morning. because you trace the bones that make up my body and that make up my chemistry. and honestly you call me the moon, the sun, and all of the stars and you say you used to wish on those stars, but when you are with me you do not need to. and that is beautiful. and i never want us to end. just tell me we will never end, i do not want you to be my supermarket lover."
"we will never end."
"promise?"
"i promise."

dancers were never my type anyway

you are not a dancer
and i understand that it is because your body
does not move fluidly
the way a ballerina seems to change with the wind,
but tell me,
how can that be
when all you do
is dance through my head?
a beautiful melody
of words
and laughter
and images
and you
and you
and you
and always you.

you say you are not a dancer,
but dancers were never my type anyway.

the darkest nights are nothing when i am with you

he held me in his arms
and he whispered in a voice no louder
than a hush,
"you do it."
i sighed: "what do you mean?"
"i mean you do it. i do not know how you do it but you do it. every
single day you wake up and you are so strong, you are so strong."
he repeated himself, as if trying to show the importance.
"you are so strong. you deserve the world.
you deserve the galaxy
and you deserve ten thousand galaxies
and you deserve the universe
and you deserve it all.
you deserve so much more that i could give to you and i am sorry i
only have a dimly lit star but it is all that i have and if i get more i
will give you more but all i have is this."
and that was the first night i cried in front of him
my thoughts kept venturing to how tight he was hugging me:
was he trying to put me together?
or was he fearing i would fall apart?
either way
he deserves the same.

two ships, neither one sinking

if you are a disease
i never want to be able to find a cure;
if you are a roadblock
i will make sure to go through your detour.

if you are medication
i want to feel all of the side effects;
if you are damaged
i want you to make me part of all the rejects.

if you are rain
i want to be guaranteed i will drown in you;
if you are nothing but a stranger
i am going to be remembered as someone you knew.

because if you are you
i want to be the only one kissing your lips;
if you are you
i will never be a sinking ship.

for my parents

i think i fell in love with you
at the start of november,
but rainy days melt as one
and honestly i do not remember.
we were fourteen but all i hoped was one day
you and i would be together.

i guess you fell in love with me
towards the end of november,
you looked me in the eyes
in that moment, my name i could not remember,
all i knew was you said
we would always be together.

then snowy days came
and suddenly it was the end of december,
you looked me in the eyes and laughed
"we will always be together,"
our love was perfectly steady
not changing like the weather.

months turned to years
and suddenly it was the seventh december,
this entire time, you and i
had, like you promised, always been together,
and we took a trip for two
to a place with "better weather."

i think i fell in love with you
at the start of a november,
and you fell in love with me
right before december,
when you got down on one knee
i knew my life would always get better.

the whole town came to our wedding
in the middle of december,
the snow outside piled up high
like our love we felt together,
and it had fulfilled your promise:
we were now together forever.

and years passed by
and us and our children grew together,
the love in our household
was always getting better and better,
and we showed them our legacy:
love will always last forever.

and i know one day
even if we are not together,
death may part us
but we will always be remembered,
because you made me feel something
full of sweeter, grandeur splendor.

but we will live on
and our children's love will last forever,
and even in stormy days
in the worst of the possible weather,
we will be recalled,
for the two who fell in love together.

these are a few of my favorite things

it is the center of the universe
and the way metal rusts,
it is the wave of the ocean
and the security of stardust;
it is the sound of the wind
and the color of the dark,
it is the warmth of a fire
and how it begins with a spark;
it is the wide-open fields
and the vastness of outer space,
it is the silent libraries
and the serenity of your warm embrace;
it is the wavelength of violet
and the rain in a storm,
it is the static kisses
and the shiver in the warm;
it is the intensity of the darkest night
and of the reddest sunset
it is the way our muscles contract
and our minds never forget;
it is the reverberations
and the echoes in the valleys,
it is the unspoken truths inside
artists and their galleries;
it is the way the first snow
retraces steps to the last winter,
it is the sainthood
behind every single sinner;
it is the wind billowing
and it is the summer rain,
it is the window seat
next to the wing of a plane;
but mainly it is you, it is you
and your hair and your everything,
and it is you and it is you
no matter what the future brings;
it is you.
it has always been
and it will always be
you.

the seasons and you

you said
the closest   <u>season</u>
        to your
                demeanor
            was   ~~winter~~:
    frigid   cold
            *light*less,
            *life*less
            and   ~~bitter~~;
        but
even if   your soul
        is the
            winter solstice
    that is ~~okay~~;
        because   i like
            winter
            better than <u>spring</u>
────────────── ~~anyway~~.

part six;

love and other words you created new definitions for

acquiver (adj.)
\ə'quiver\

1.   shaking or trembling because of strong emotion; quivering;
2.   i used to think that the only things that would cause me to tremble were my biggest fears: heights, losing people i loved, claymation movies, and spiders. but you showed me differently. the day you first looked into my eyes i felt my body shake just a little. even if it was a little, it was enough to make me realize that i moved in some way. connotations surrounding trembling were always negative and showed something bad. but that day, the exact opposite of something bad happened. i used to think that by "strong emotion," the definition referred to fear;
3.   maybe it means love.

dulcet (adj.)
/ˈdəlsit/

1.   sweet, soothing, sugary;
2.   i do not have a sweet tooth. and all my friends and all of my family laugh at me because i was never a big fan of halloween, i never had dessert unless it was tart and i would kindly say "no thank you" when presented a sugary delight in front of me. but my palate changed since we met. everything about you was sweet, everything about you was dulcet: honestly i fell for your eyes before anything else and they were the deepest brown i have ever looked into and they were like some form of milk chocolate and so i went home and destroyed a bag of hershey kisses. and your warm embrace baked me like a cookie and you smelled like vanilla. next thing i knew, your kiss had me longing for some sugary delights and your touch had me tasting candy. i am at the point where i do not care if you give me a cavity, i would rather die from the taste of your sweetness then live a life without tasting it again. because you are the cure to all of my diseases and the side effects to all of which i believe in, you and your sugary soul.

fausse nostalgie (adj.)
/fòs` - no stɐl gē/

1. false or untrue nostalgia, usually brought upon when
    something has not happened but it feels like it has;
2. "i want to meet you" you say;
3. "i feel like i already know you, like i have known you for
    the past two years of my life. like i know your friends and
    your body and i know your mind and your soul; i know your
    hands and the color of your cheeks when you smile and i
    know the way you laugh and i feel like i know what color
    you would choose to paint your toenails if you had the
    chance right now and i know you and i feel like i have
    known you forever." i say;
4. "i love you" you say back.

folie a deux (n.)
/fō͵ lē ä ˈdœ/

1.   a mental illness shared by two people in close association;
2.   *see love*

ineffable (adj.)
/in'efəb(ə)l/

1. too great to be fully expressed in words;
2. the only thing that ever courses through my head is you. the only thing that ever dares to escape from my mouth and my lips is your name. how does anyone expect me to function when i have become engulfed in an ocean full of thoughts of you, when i close my eyes and i see you, when i smell your scent when you are not around. *this love is truly ineffable.*

love (n., adj.)
/ˈləv/

1.   a feeling of strong or constant affection for a person
2.   the feeling or wobble in my knees i receive every single time your delicate fingers and long fingernails caress some part of my body: my hands, my thigh, my neck, even though i was never really a skin-on-skin type of person;
3.   the desire i feel to grab you by the collar and kiss you flat on your lips, hard, when your hair is shining in the moonlight and your body is a silhouette masked out by the edges of all the stars in the universe;
4.   when we drive around at some late hour of the night when most of the world is fast asleep and we roll down all of the windows no matter the temperature is outside and we turn the music up as loud as we can and we scream songs and get engulfed in words and we take the long way home to talk about the universe;
5.   when you tickle me so hard i can't breathe and i tell you to stop, i tell you it over and over again, but you never stop and instead tell me i have an intoxicating laugh, you tell me that it makes you high, and instead of stopping you tell me that my smile is a disease and you are completely engulfed by the existence of the disease and you love it, you really love it. all of the symptoms, all of it. that is what love is.
6.   the dictionary definition does not do mercy to what love really is. love is love is love is love. i could go on. but why bother when i know that *what i feel for you is love*.
7.   ive found that you cannot use words to fully express your love for someone. it is a combination of this impossibility and this inexplicability that i believe fully envelopes the true definition of love: love is speechless. and perhaps if we could perfectly describe it, it would not be love.

luminescence (n.)
/lo͞omə'nesəns/

1. the creation of light by a process that does not involve heat;
2. example; *your eyes are luminescent*;
3. example; *your soul is luminescent.*

miracle (n.)
/'mēr-i-kel/

1. extraordinary event manifesting divine intervention in human affairs;
2. you said you never believed in any miracles. you said you would be an atheist if your parents did not drag you to sunday school as a child, if you did not make your confirmation and have to play the role of the "perfect catholic child" to your parents. but i just kind of laughed at you. because the earth is on the perfect tilt that if it was changed by even a fraction of a degree, the seasons would be different, the weather would be screwed up and time would be different, it might even be unsustainable for all human life. and because almost ninety percent of the ocean floor is not mapped out, meaning that there are tens of thousands of animals and plant life that will remain a mystery. because the collision of molecules in an airtight space collapsed, expanded, and created something out of nothing, rendering up all gases, which began to create rock formations, which created cells and that lead to the creation of animals, somehow, which created humans, making us born of the same dust particles as stars. because a single speck of dust created everything we have ever known. because there may be no edge to space, there may be things we will never be able to see no matter how long the earth will live, there are probably other places out there that hold some other life form. because we as humans went from computers that were two square feet wide, to computers that fit in our pockets and on our ears. because we exist. because we are alive. because there are countless things that are extraordinary in my, in this, ordinary life;
3. including you;
4. you said you did not believe in miracles. but i just kind of laughed. what about you and i meeting? what about you and i falling in love with each other?;
5. out of all of these, you are the greatest miracle to happen to me.

momentous (adj.)
/mō'men(t)əs,mə'men(t)əs/

1.   of great importance or significance;

2.   you said to me: "i have been trying to find a way to describe the way it feels to live and not just," you paused as you ran your fingers through your hair as if to emphasize the importance of your next word which you put air quotes around: "'exist' in a moment. and honestly it is because it is such a rare thing to experience. to not exist, to instead be alive. most people are just...there." you paused again. i could tell your thoughts were in a billion places at once. you bit your lip, thinking, looking somewhere to the left of my feet, and then you continued, "and i mean sure there is so much i want to say to you right now in this moment while we sit here, but i seem to not be able to function properly and formulate sentences that are grammatically and spiritually correct. but there are many moments in my life when i feel like i am alive. and honestly, they are always when i am with you. it is whenever i leave you at twelve-thirty in the morning and my sister is outside your house and when i get in the car she yells at me for making her come out so late, but i just sigh and smile and say sorry because you make me feel like i am important in your life, like i mean something to the universe. like maybe somehow it won't matter that the entire human species will one day completely die out and there will be no one left to remember the life we try so hard to build up. but God, when i talk to you i am a galaxy and not the remnants of a dead and burnt out star and i love you for that";

3.   you do not know that you are more than a galaxy;

4.   you are my universe;

5.   you are *momentous*.

selenophile (n.)
/sa-lē-no-fil/

1.   a person who loves the moon;
2.   when i first met you, you told me that the moon was your
      favorite object in the universe and that you thought i was
      beautiful because you saw two moons in my eyes;
3.   when we fell together we created our very own universe.

somnambulist (n.)
/säm-ˈnam-byə-ˌli-st/

1.   a sleepwalker;
2.   when people ask me what i like about you i do not usually mention those hazel eyes full of poetry or your soul of sweet music. i say that you talk in your sleep. i say that you are a sleepwalker and talker. because when we fall asleep arm in arm, hand in hand, soul intertwined with broken soul, you never fail to wake me up with some words muttered. and the one i remember most was the first night i realized you talked in your sleep: we were talking about the universe before we fell asleep as you traced pictures on my face and you kissed my neck and my back. and it was probably two in the morning when i woke up and i heard you say that the aliens were coming and i gave a little giggle and then a little sigh and i said, "shut up, go back to sleep" and you did not reply you just kept talking and you said "no" a few times and by the time i realized you were asleep you got up out of bed and you walked into the bathroom and i followed you in, knowing you were sleepwalking and you just kept banging your head against the wall and muttering "i am so stupid" and when i asked what was wrong you said "i never got to tell you i loved you and now the aliens are here";
3.   when i got you back into bed i kissed you on your forehead and i saw you smile and that is when i knew sleepwalker or not, i was unfathomably in love with every single piece of you.

supine (adj.)
/soo- pīn/

1.   lying face upwards;
2.   when we count the stars at night and try to find as many constellations as we can;
3.   when we cuddle up close and next to each other on the couch under a blanket and i hold your hand and you hold mine and we talk and laugh and i kiss your nose;
4.   when you and i watch a movie together, but get too caught up in each other to know what is happening to any of the characters;
5.   when i call you at night, and i know on the other end you are on speaker phone and you are probably staring up towards your ceiling and you are probably in a white shirt, because what else would you be doing, what else would you be wearing?;
6.   when we play scrabble and you get mad because i always beat you so you throw the board and the pieces and then i make you collect them and every single time that happens, we end up playing with the letters on the ground;
7.   when i fall asleep in your bed and you are next to me.

syzygy (n.)
/ˈsi-ze-jē/

1. the nearly straight-line configuration of three celestial bodies in a gravitational system;
2. when your body is not intertwined with me, but instead when you and i are walking towards each other and i see you and you see me and we stop walking and just stare at each other for a few seconds, our eyes locked, smiles beginning to form on each of our faces, until the gravity becomes too much, the pressure begins to form in my head, and i drop whatever is in my hands and run after you, as you do the same on the other side of the room. we begin as a syzygy. we end as the collision of molecules, but not a black hole. the big bang, not the destruction of matter. and it is beautiful.

part seven;

entropy and other words you gave new definitions for

brood (n.)
/bro͞od/

1. to think about something that makes one unhappy;
2. I cannot believe that you are now gone. i cannot believe that you are now leaving me. i cannot believe that at one point you told me that i was your future and there was nothing else you pictured in your life but me. now you are gone;
3. you are my *brood* and i do not even care to know that that is not a grammatically correct sentence. you are my unhappy thing. you are my captivating thought of destruction.

eloquence (n.)
/e-lə-kwən(t)s/

1. the ability to speak or write in a well and effective way;
2. i used to always tell you that you would make it as an author, that your writing was good enough to be published, but i change my mind. i think you deserve to be a playwright. not only should you write the scripts you create, but you should also act in the plays. i have never met anyone as well-rounded in all the worst ways except for you. you spoke so eloquently that i was drawn to you in so many ways. your words made me fall in love with you. but your empty words made me want to leave you.

entropy (n.)
/ˈen-trə-pē/

1. the inadequacy to produce enough mechanical work in thermodynamics, which is interpreted as a series of randomness or organized chaos;
the lack of order; disorder;

2. the way that i can taste whoever else's lips have been on your lips other than my own, the flavor of cherries still resides in my mind that one day i kissed you like i hadn't seen you in forever but backed away at the first taste of cherries. when i asked you, you said that you put on chap stick because your lips were dry, your lips "always get dry especially in the winter," and so we laughed about it even though you said it was embarrassing. in hindsight i guess i should've seen it coming because looking back at it now i am laughing for being stupid enough to believe that your lips get chapped in the winter. i was stupid enough to believe you. and then when i kissed you a few weeks later and was able to taste coconut on your lips i didn't say anything because i knew it then. i knew it the second our lips locked on that january day. but i didn't want to believe that you were shallow enough to have someone else in your life. so i gave you a second chance. but every single time my leg brushed up against yours i couldn't stand to think that there was another person touching the very same leg. and when your fingers caressed me, when they danced on my arm, i didn't want your fingerprints staining me any more than they already were. and when you talk to me at night and you tell me what i mean to you, when you whisper sweet nothings into my ear and tell me things i only wished for in my wildest dreams, i do not want to think about it, but you probably had recycled your words, had rewound yourself, had twisted the pole that stuck out of your back so you talked the same words again like a toy, like one of those old string toys, in the monotony of your voice, no emotion was ever put into loving me. because we are walking on ice that is cracking under our feet and you remain calm in a time of total and absolute disarray and we are falling down into an era of not gradual but total and sudden outbursts of disorder.

ephemeral (adj.)
/i-ˈfem-rəl/

1.   lasting for a short time;
2.   funny. you said forever. you held my hand and you said
forever. you kissed my lips and said you never wanted to
taste anything else but them. you said they were sweeter
than anything you have ever tasted and you have never
wanted to taste anything else but my lips. you said we
would break up when the stars and the moon collide, when
the earth somehow becomes swallowed up by a giant black
hole that NASA never saw coming, when there is a giant
asteroid that comes crashing down into earth and all who
inhabit it are swallowed up by the darkness and destruction
it left. well, i guess the end of the world is here;
3.   us.

fugacious (adj.)
/fō`gä- shus/

1.   disappearing, fleeting;

i never thought we would fall out of love. i never thought you would cheat on me and fall in love with someone else. i never thought your mind would be full of someone else and mine would still be captivated on you. i never thought any of this would happen but i mean now you are gone and now the feeling we felt together is gone and now you are gone and now you are gone and now you are gone and now you are gone and i do not know what to do and now you are gone and now you are gone and now you are gone and now you are gone and now you are gone and i do not know what to do and now you are gone and now you are gone and now you are gone and now you are gone and now you are gone and i do not know what to do and now you are gone and now you are gone and now you are gone and now you are gone and i do not know what to do and now you are gone and now you are gone and now you are gone and now you are gone and now you are gone and i do not know what to do and now you are gone and now you are gone and now you are gone and now you are gone and i do not know what to do and now you are gone and now you are gone and now you are gone and now you are gone and now you are gone and i do not know what to do and now you are gone and now you are gone and now you are gone and now you are gone and now you are gone and now you are gone and now you are gone and now you are gone

hiraeth (n.)
/he`reth/

1. a homesickness for a place that was never your home; a
homesickness for a home you cannot return to;
2. you broke my heart but all i want is nothing more than to
have your arms around my hips and your lips against my
skin. you were one of the only things in my life that was
constant, one of the only things in my life that meant
something and i am so homesick for arms that are not mine
anymore and i am so homesick for arms i can never have
again and i am homesick for arms that have freckles really
close to the underside of the elbow where i would always
fall asleep and i am homesick for arms that have a tattoo on
the left bicep, a single latin word that i do not even
remember and i bet it never even mattered but all i know is
that you were drunk when you got the tattoo and it is funny
and it was cute but i am homesick for those arms.

inauspicious (adj.)
/ˌinôˈspiSHəs/

1. unsuccessful, unlucky;
2. "you know that feeling when you fall on cement or concrete
and you hit your hands and you look to see if you are
bleeding but it just hurts, it really hurts?" you nodded so i
continued, tears beginning to form on the corners of my
eyes, "and then you squeeze it, you know you should not
but you do, you squeeze it and the blood then comes? and
you think to yourself 'boy am i so unlucky?' that is always
how i felt when i was around you. when you would kiss me
or your hand would be placed perfectly in mine or when you
would touch the inside of my leg or play with my hair, i felt
both of my knees grow weak. i thought it was out of love.
but it was not. it was much more. i would look down and
see myself bleeding, i would see bruises all along the sides
of my arms and on my face and i thought, 'well, what a
cruel and unlucky way to go. the one you love being the
reason for your death.' and i would cry and i would scream
and i would wish for you to come back or i would wish for
us to have never met because i loved you more than
anything but to you, i do not know what i was. you never
even loved me, did you?" you did nothing but stare at me
with an open mouth and then i saw you begin to cry, but
you turned around and i got what i wanted: you were gone.

nefarious (adj.)
/nə ˈferēəs/

1.   wicked, evil, criminal;
2.   there are countless amounts of words to describe you and among those, many include evil;
3.   i cannot believe you cheated on me. i cannot believe you cheated on me. i cannot believe you cheated on me. i cannot believe you cheated on me. you are evil, you are *nefarious*, you are wicked, you are criminal, you are sick, you are horrible, you are you but you are horrible you are you but you are sick. you are you and i am me. you are fire and i am water. you are death and i am life. you are poison and i am a flower;
4.   you are you;
5.   and i am me;
6.   and we can never work out because of who we are.

phosphenes (n.)
/ˈfäs-ˌfēn/

1. a luminous impression due to the excitation of the retina;
   2. seeing lights that aren't really there;
3. looks are deceiving. i saw a light in you, a light that went out almost as fast as i saw it. not all that glitters is gold and not all things that shine are light. i see that now;
   4. *you.*

superfluous (adj.)
/soo͞ˈpərflōo͞əs/

1.   unnecessary, especially through being more than enough;
2.   i always thought we would somehow end up together. i thought you were my destiny, my love undying, my lover forever. but you were just a heart murmur i recovered from. i always thought you were enough for me, enough for me to love, enough for me to feel loved, enough for forever. and we did not fall apart because you were not enough. we fell apart because you were too much. it is like i was a fire just meant to keep people warm and you were buckets of gasoline. we destroyed ourselves and we destroyed people around us and we destroyed each other.

veracity (adj.)
/vəˈrasədē/

1. the accuracy or the truthfulness
2. the truth? do you want the truth? okay well the truth is i love you and i hate myself every single day for it. i hate myself for loving you because you are such bad news and you have been bad news ever since you came hurtling like an asteroid into my life. the truth is that even though you hurt me so bad that my soul has now become past the point of being broken and has ventured into an era of becoming shattered, i still think of you. and every once in a while, i pass your street and i think of turning and knocking on your door. or i find something in the store that i think you would like and i pick it up and i almost think about buying it but i never do. or i listen to a song that you played for me and even though i know all of the words, i do not sing. the truth is i am in love with you. even after you hurt me so bad. the truth is i do not know when i will stop loving you. the truth is i love you so much and i do not know when i will stop loving you. the truth is i love you and i hate myself every single day because of it.

part eight;

midnight conversations with my pillow //
the drunk words i sometimes slur

ashes to gold

from dead to reincarnate
      from lost to found;
      from calm to irate
      and floating to drowned.

you change and bend
      but you never, ever break;
      you climb and ascend
      but you never, ever ache.

from flame to fire
      from dizzy to sane;
      from calm to dire
      and sunny to rain.

you live to go higher
      but you never go down;
      you live to be a fighter
      but you never lose the crown.

from ignorance to finesse
      from bought to sold;
      from regress to progress
      and ashes to gold.

i (love/hate) myself

honestly it is like i am broken
and i do not want to be fixed;
like i am on choppy water
and my boat will be the first to sink.

and i have been numb so long
i forgot what it meant to feel;
i have been dreaming for too long
i do not know what is fiction and what is real.

it is like my days are falling apart
but i do not try to get them back together;
my head is full of bruised thoughts
and i will never get better.

i have been gone for so long
i do not think i am ever coming back;
and i have been living in muted colors
in shades of white and black.

it is like i have a lethal disease
and medication does not alleviate pain;
my skull is full of emptiness
and echoes stream through my veins.

i have been watching the sky for so long
i forgot to look down on the ground;
i have been lost for forever
and i will never be found.

i do not know who i am
but i do not care enough to know;
i hate being by myself
it is the only person that will never go.

the story of my thoughts on god and the universe
thursday, july 18, 2014
01:43

her name was annabeth. she was my first love.

she was blonde and had brown eyes which was a mix i had never witnessed before, but nonetheless she was absolutely beautiful, the prettiest girl i had ever seen. she wore flowers in her hair to counteract the starlit constellations that formed in her mind.
our love story was pretty typical, pretty predictable, regardless, it was pretty damn pretty.

but i do not want to focus on our love story, i want to talk about our heartbreak.

we broke up because of a fight. i cannot tell you what it was about, i mean i do not remember: it was years and years ago, but what would two sixteen-year olds not fight about, we fought about life and its meaning and about the color of the universe and the reason why humans have tailbones.

i loved that about us. not the fact we fought, but the fact that we talked about everything. we did not discuss the way that alcohol stings our throats after each sip at a party with music too loud for our ears to handle; we talked about english literature and about the books that make us laugh or the ones that make us cry and the songs that we listen to when we felt alone.

"i hate you, i hate everything about you, i never want to see you again," she said to me behind tears while she tried to run and i grabbed her wrist to pull her back towards me.

i tried to keep my cool, but my voice was yelling subconsciously, "you know you need me to live. i know you need me to live. so why are you going to leave me? why? what did i do to you that made you feel this way because honestly i could work on it, honestly i could change myself to make you love me."

she backed away a little bit: "okay do you not see how stupid that sounds? do you not realize how horrible that is? you want to change yourself just to have me. that is not love. that is nowhere close to what love is. love is changing things like the fact that you do not put down the toilet seat after peeing or always forgetting to close the refrigerator, not your entire personality. you can not change that about yourself. you cannot change the fact that you think the way you think. you can not change yourself. and i am sorry, i really am, but i cannot have you because i cannot change the desires i have in my life and the fact that out of all those desires, you are not included. i cannot change the fact that when i talk about the things i love, you are on that list and so is God and so is the universe and stardust and the letter v and record players but i am not. i cannot change the fact that you do not know what you did to me and honestly i do not know what you did either but all i know is when i am around somehow i am the devil and you are the godliest god and everything i do is wrong. i am sorry for doing this to you and i am sorry for telling your mom i was in love with you last week but next week she will not know why i can never say your name the same way again without thinking of saying goodbye. i am sorry for everything i have done, but mostly i am really, really sorry for everything i should have done but failed to do."

she never kissed me goodnight that day and the next day she picked up all the things that were stuffed into my drawers. but lately i have been cleaning up and today, two weeks after breaking up with her, i found the stub of the ticket we used to get into a concert she begged me to go to with her. so i texted her and asked if she still wanted it and she said yes and i told her i would give it to her when i saw her in school the next day. and she never replied back but i have been thinking and i cannot imagine where i would be if it was not for her soul of pure stardust and if it were not for her dragging me to church every single sunday with her mother and brother and how after each procession we would get bagels and she would always get bacon, egg, and cheese on an everything bagel and i would get scallion cream cheese on a plain bagel and we always asked if they could slice the bagels in half so we could split them. i do not know where i would be if it was not for her telling me one night everything she believed in and you can say that either i was in love and naive or i was stupid and unconditionally reproachable, but all i know is that she said she believed in God. she believed in everything the Bible said but she did not believe in adam and eve.

she did believe in evolution and natural selection and she believed in the big bang. she told me that "the universe could not have been created by a god who was bored of darkness and so he created light," she turned toward me in the car while we were atop some mountain overlooking the city lights, "do you get what i mean? i mean i believe in predestination and that my prayers are getting to a heavenly person, but i do not think that the universe was created in a week. i do not think that on the first day light was created and then the earth and then everything on it. i believe that the first things ever were protons and neutrons that created light and then from those protons and neutrons, the first traces of stars and asteroids began to be created. and countless crashes later, the earth was created. you get it?" i nodded in agreement.

and now i believe in the same things. i believe what she told me she believes in. i believe in everything. and long story short, i have been avoiding her in the hallways and i still have the ticket from that night somewhere in my room pinned up on one of my cork walls.

her name was annabeth. she was my first love. and she was my first heartbreak.

our love story was typical, our demise was beautiful.

i want to (die/live) i do not want to (die/live)
sunday, november 20, 2013
00:27

i just want to die, i do not want to keep on living;
there is no point to moving on, i have not found a reason to keep
giving.
i just want to get out, find my way from this eternal darkness;
people say that i am so cold, they call me nothing but mean and
heartless.

i just want to die, i have not found a reason to keep on living;
people keep on hurting me, i am so done with forgiving.
i just want to leave this world, get out of my body and my head;
there is no point to living in color when all i see is red.

but i will never see the sunset against the silhouette of my beautiful
baby;
i will never pick out the flowers, see her hair full of daisies.
i just want to fall asleep while we stare up into the sky;
i want to keep living, i never want to die.

and i will never become one with whom i was meant to be;
i will never see the things i have always wanted to see.
i just want to move forward and never have to say goodbye;
i want to keep living, i never want to die.

the hardest thing

sometimes the feeling is burning
like a forest fire underneath my skin
and i spark and burn.
other times it is a candle
barely taking in enough oxygen
to keep itself alive.
yet either way it is there;
burning,
burning,
burning
for you.
it sucks without you here:
there is no poetic way
to describe the sadness
that comes without having you
but still loving you.

advice from my freshmen and sophomore math teacher

i had the same math teacher in freshmen year as i did sophomore year, and on the first day of my high school career, as i stepped into her algebra two class after the bell rang, she said with a smile, "**this is the hardest math class you have ever taken**." and i did not give a second thought to that.

then, sophomore year, i stepped through the same classroom doors taking pre-calculus and she smiled and said again, "**this is the hardest math class you have ever taken**." and after sitting on that statement for this long i have come to realize maybe she was not just talking about math:

for example, i fell in love with a girl once with blue hair whose name started with the same letter as her favorite color, but funny how i remember neither. maybe alexa and auburn. but she said she loved me after three months of talking and i told her i loved her too. but suddenly she left for reasons i do not even remember, but i bet it was stupid. and i was distraught, depressed, and dissatisfied with everything. i thought that was the lowest point in my life. **that was the hardest math class i had ever taken.**

but then two years later i witnessed things that affect me to this day, i witnessed murder and suicide and loss and tears and i witnessed saying goodbye to people i love and i lost my best friend to something terrible and my great grandmother died and my dad lost his job and my family was in this perpetual state of amnesia where we could not even remember to say goodnight to each other and the words "i love you" were rarely ever muttered and it is truly sad to think that the people i loved were the people who were leaving faster than ever and i **realized that was the hardest math class i had ever taken.**

and we say we want things simpler and we look to the past for that simplicity and in two years i know life will become even sluttier and screw me over yet again and i will think back to the time i loved a girl whose hair was blue and whose eyes matched her soul and i will think about how stupid i was to think that her leaving was the end of the world. but we always tend **to take harder math classes as the years go on.**

how sad, all my best friends are miles and miles away

the beginning of the calamitous feeling seems to sink in:
i can conjure your fingerprints in my mind,
but i will never fully understand the feeling of your skin.

i can envision the look in your deep beautiful eyes,
and listen to music that reminds me of you,
but nothing compares to the actual feeling of the inside of your thigh.

i can stimulate my senses to distinguish who you are
and replay memories of seeing you in my dreams,
but you will not come even if every day i wish on these stars.

i can pretend to know the taste of your ambrosial lips,
and create endless fairytales where one day we meet,
but funny how someone i do not know is someone i miss.

"ask me something, make me think."
"if you cannot see something, is it really there?"

this echoes the phrase that goes: if a tree falls in the forest, with no
one there to witness it, does it make a sound?
the answer is yes, put simply.
so if you cannot see something, is it really there?
the answer again is yes, put simply.
for example: gravity, nuclear forces, magnetics, molecular attraction,
and many other fundamental scientific principles and ideologies.
for example: the radio, micro, sound, color, ultraviolet, and infrared
waves.
for example: trust.
for example: faith.
for example: love and personal attraction.
just because you cannot see something, it does not mean it is not
there.
just look at the sky, the atmosphere,
and the planets orbiting the sun.
just feel the wind
just feel the heart beating in your chest.
just feel the earth moving.
just look at you
and just look at me
and look at everything.
just because you cannot see something, it does not mean it is not
there.
just look at you
and just look at me
and the love we have for each other.

a beneficial sacrifice

he would lay down on her chest
until she was unable to breathe
and only when he got up did she see:
sometimes the people you love
are the ones that need to leave.

my own proverb

if you fall
enjoy the view:
the stars
are more visible
when your back
is in mud.

bad habits

he clenched his jaw with each lie he told.
that was one of the first things i learned about him.
we were standing in his kitchen one day, my hand placed delicately
within his own skin, touching softly. his mom was cooking dinner.
"is it okay if we go to jessica's for dinner? it will be us and a few
friends," he asked,
when in reality our hangout consisted of going to the park.
his mom turned to him, stopped and looked up from the stove that
had pasta cooking.
she turned right back, stirring the pot with a wooden spoon.
"you are lying, where are you going?" she saw right past his lie.
"no i am not lying mom, we are going to jess's! you want to call her
parents?" he lied again.
his mom now turned to face me:
"sweetie," she started, "whenever he lies his jaw locks and unlocks a
few times. just look at his chin now."
i turned to him, but he suddenly became self-conscious and i watched
him unclench his jaw.
"it may come in handy one day" and she was back to stirring her
pasta, offering me one quick wink.

two years later we were standing in the park,
his hand around my waist,
my eyes stained with tears caused by no one but him.
"i still love you" he said.
some bad habits are never broken:
his jaw was clenched.

i never got to thank his mom.

a soul shooting

i wore a bulletproof jacket
whenever i was around you;
for i feared you would take
the gun of your mouth
and find a way to shoot me
directly in the heart;
but then you smiled,
told me how much you loved me
and pulled the trigger
when the gun
was pointed at my head.

built to fall apart

our love was a castle--
a monument with no cement:
we built ourselves up,
but fell apart without intent.

*what my old friend once told me after i lost someone i loved to
someone else*

every single person in the world has a key, figuratively, of course.
and every single person in the world has a locked heart.
if you have ever seen the way a lock works, you know that the key
needs to be a perfect fit in order for the door to open.
this is the exact same way humans love.
some people just do not fit together.
some people fall out of love fast because it is obvious from the start
that the key that someone else has is nowhere near the makeup of
their heart.
some people spend their entire life in love with someone who holds a
key so close to that of their heart, they think they are the one they are
supposed to be with forever.
some people shove their key into someone else's heart and all they
want is for the key to fit, that is all we ever want, the key to just fit.
but
maybe falling in love
and then falling out of it
is not a bad thing.
think about it:
every single time you fall in love and then fall out of love, you are
one person closer to finding the love of your life, you are one step
closer to meeting the person who will fulfill your dreams, the one
who will make you feel what it means to be in love.
every single heartbreak
is a step forward
even if your world feels like it is falling
down.
because every single heartbreak
is every single key
not made for your heart.
so maybe
falling out of love
is just as important
as what it means to fall in love.

i am lost somewhere in outer space

though the slightest wind moves me from my feet,
and these hurricanes make me feel complete;
i may be in pain, but i know these times will move on:
the darkness may show but i will survive until dawn.

i know the worst troubles will always get better
even in the worst forms of the stormiest weather;
these sounds of lightning and these visions of thunder
pour down like the rain that i will never fall under.

because here in this life, it is mine for the taking,
here in this life, it is all of which i make it;
so i will move on, this darkness will somehow turn to light,
and like a star i will shine through the night.

and although i am stumbling through outer space,
i will always surpass a newfound grace;
and so i will sail on, this boat against a stormy current,
and i will move on: for this, i am determined.

you were oxygen and i was a candle. you left and i burned out.

water begins to boil at one hundred degrees celsius and the slightest
bit of water is needed to make a candle completely disappear. but
there has to be an equilibrium where the heat of the candle makes the
water evaporate, but the water makes the candle go out.
i think that was you and me.
we hurt each other
more than we ever helped.
and honestly it sucks that our entire relationship
was built off of this tiered monarchal bigotry destined to topple over
after just one mistake.
and i fell in love with you
because you kept me alive;
but is that love?
is this love?
were we love?
you were oxygen and you left and i burned out and i honestly do not
know where i would be without you but i do not know if i would
happier if you were not with me anymore.
and i was fire and you were water and i made you leave, i drove you
to the point of leaving me.
you left and you were gone and i loved you and i lost you and now
that
you are gone,
so
am
i.

a walk with my emotions

i fell in love with Happiness.
she owned each beat of my pure heart.
a metronome circulating love and joy:
Happiness was mine from the start.

i seemed to smile constantly,
she said i radiated heat and warmth.
as long as Happiness loved me, and i, her,
you can say i was the happiest man on earth.

i grasped onto Happiness loosely,
for i never thought i would lose her hold;.
but she left when she got the chance:
my once bright life was suddenly cold.

darkness poured into my life,
black sunlight seemed to surround me.
Happiness was nowhere to be found,
i did not know where i was meant to be.

i walked alone for quite some time
ever since Happiness decided to vanish.
but then i saw a girl in the road
and that is how i fell in love with Sadness.

Sadness held onto me rather tightly
slowly she began to take control.
she did not love me, she bruised me:
she tainted my heart and broke my soul.

Sadness was an awful puppeteer,
and i acted as her lawful marionette.
i had gotten so attached to Sadness,
Happiness was a name I seemed to forget.

i ran away from my sudden captive
and broke loose of the ropes on my back.
i thought i would be okay without her,
but my already dark life seemed to turn jet black.

i was a migrant, a traveller; no love, no home.
Sadness was gone, but Happiness was, too.
i lived an abandoned life, a prisoner to thoughts,
saw no colors but every single shade of blue.

unbecoming me became a slave to my emotions,
i gained absolutely no reason to be here.
no one to love me but my emotions:
i found comfort in Jealousy, Doubt, and Fear.

they controlled me, they destroyed me;
each one, a different, negative feeling.
they hurt me, i felt them all:
though i was not cut i found myself bleeding.

though i thought they restrained me
i was always in control of my emotions:
i grabbed the life vest in front of me,
departed the glass waves of the ocean.

there was Happiness all along:
within my body and capturing my soul.
she loved me even though i pushed her away.
Happiness was my home.

Happiness built me up,
i was the one to knock myself down.
i had blamed my depression on Sadness,
but she did not have the crown.

i let Sadness consume me,
when i could have left at any moment.
i thought my heart was hurt,
but it was me, the one who broke it.

i laughed at myself,
i was so stupid for being so sad.
i smiled instead,
i told myself to be glad.

so i took a stroll with Sadness.
we held hands for quite some time.
she came to terms with my new lover:
Happiness was once again mine.

drowning in regret

and at the end of the night
you look back on all of the times
you could have said something
but you just sit on your bed
tracing constellations in your thoughts
and creating false hopes
and realities that can never exist
so you think to yourself
"am i really living"
and no matter how hard you try,
you are unable to come up
with a proper answer;
for your mind has let go
but your fingers can never forget:
so you drown in bottles upon bottles
until your drown in your regret.

i am getting better

the day i replaced the thought
of negativity in my head with ones
that instead created joy,
i became better.

the day i stopped thinking
of all of the evil in the world,
but instead of what i could do to change it,
i became better.

the day i stopped wondering
what it would be like to be happy
and instead produced my own light,
i became better.

and even though i am not there yet,
and golden does not describe my days
of thoughtless, colorless blurs;
i am getting better.

ever since that night

he said he lived in darkness
ever since he drowned me
in all of his golden light.
when he gave me life
his perfect eyes turned starless
and something in him changed
ever since that night.

the difference between love and loss

"love scares the absolute shit out of me"

"why?"

"because it always ends, it always ends in heartbreak and sadness and i am done."

"it does not always end in heartbreak. what about marriage?"

"you are right. i just want to skip ahead until i meet the person i know i am going to marry. at least then i know it will never end. do you feel that way?"

"no i do not. i mean, sure it would be great to skip ahead and know who you are going to marry. but i do not want that to happen to me. i would rather suffer a thousand heartbreaks than find out who i am going to marry."

"why?"

"because there is a blatant difference between those two types of loves. i want to know what it is like to love only skin deep, only on the surface, not even touching my heart. i want to know what it is like to never think about the person i 'love' and i want to bawl my eyes out over worthless people. because at least then when i get married i will know what it is like to really love. i will know what it means to fall asleep with hands intertwined, and wake up with souls intertwined. i will know what it means to actually love and not just feel."

"i hate you."

"why?"

"you always give the best advice."

part nine;

*love, heartbreak, physics, other scientific facts, and reasons why
astronomy is the discovery of the soul, not the universe*

newton's laws of motion; the rules of love

I.   an object in motion tends to stay in motion unless acted on by an outside force; an object at rest tends to remain in this state until acted on by an outside force. i fell in love with a girl senior year of high school when my mind was focused on college and on my future, but i still somehow managed to think of her; taylor, i think that was her name, she was tall with brown hair that ombred into the prettiest blonde. at one point, my heart was as still as the ground beneath my feet. but in due time, as taylor began to take up more and more room in my head clogged with ideas of the future, my heart gained motion and it began to spin around and it began to gain momentum and no amount of inertia was enough to stop it. taylor was the reason my heart was set into motion. and an object at motion stays in motion. my heart, my soul, my body, my mind: all placed into the slightest bit of motion that gradually toppled into a monsoon of emotion. but newton's law holds true. taylor was the reason my heart was set into motion but taylor was the reason my heart hit a wall and stopped. outside forces are harder to recognize if they are already inside of you.

II.   for every action, there is an equal and opposite reaction: even when i loved you. my entire heart was placed carefully yet carelessly into you. and you never even looked at me.

III. f=ma: the exertion of the force of any object can be determined by multiplying the mass and acceleration together. take you and i for an example, my weight was not that which can be given by standing on a scale, instead it was given by the way that i weighed myself down with this dwindling supply of air so i was constantly reaching for something that was never coming; i was weighed down by the heaviness of living. you lifted up some of that weight when you came into my life, you almost seemed to counteract all of which i placed fondly onto myself. your happiness and your carefully carefree love was enough to lift most, but not all, of my weight. multiply that by the acceleration of me falling for you, falling long, hard, and fast, for the stardust that makes you up. i expired myself into an era of outbursts, not gradual, but those which were sudden, sporadically thinking about nothing but you. and let's just say, when these are multiplied together, love really is a great enough force to knock down walls and unlock doors.

$G=(m1xm2)/r^2$

gravity is a constant nine-point-eight meters per second squared. no matter how large of a body an object has, no matter how tiny the diameter of an object is, in any vacuum of space, they will fall and land at the same time with an acceleration of nine-point-eight meters per second. the gravitational pull between two objects (that is, the force which gravity exerts between two objects) is given in the formula equivalent to the mass of one object times the mass of another divided by the distance between the two points. so multiply together a broken heart, a bottle of vodka which was later thrown against the wall and shattered all over the hardwood floor, little drops pouring out, a puddle forming beneath; a heavy mind that seems to constantly tear me down to tiny bite sized pieces (no wonder you enjoyed my mind); a ringing in my ears from all the screaming my insides have done. and take into account the words you speak, the holes in your heart which should have made you weigh less, but instead you seemingly weighed more, the emptiness and unnecessary, uncaring, and under developed mass you call a mind, full of selfish ways. divide this, then, by the distance you emancipated between us two, the many, many miles you put between us through stupid lies and petty wrongdoings, through not being there when i needed you most, when you said you would be there for me but never were, and your unforgivable and unforgettable mistakes which leave me stranded on an island of my very own. that is the tiniest number divided by the largest on squared: so, in other words, this gravity should feel like nothing, but somehow i feel everything.

$V_{esc} = [sqrtr(2GM)] \div r$

all bodies, no matter how grand in sheer vastness or miniscule in unmistakable size, exert gravity. anything from a photon, to a pen, to the body reading this now; but gravity is usually correlated to stars or bodies in the sky. a certain velocity is needed to escape these masses. this is calculated by taking two and multiplying it by the gravitational pull by two objects (see formula above) and the mass of the object trying to escape and then dividing it by its radius. for pens, it is easy to just walk away, as they release barely any gravitational pull (see formula above). but for you, things were rather different. to escape you, i needed to gather an incomprehensible speed: two times the gravitational pull that dragged me towards you whenever you walked into the room. it seemed as if i used to call you my world, you were my everything, you were my world, and now you were as large as this "world" i called you. gravity travelled towards you, my eyes magnified towards you, my body pulled towards yours and i could not help myself from doing it. multiply this, then, by your mass, your egotistical and narcissistic head, filling up your entire body, the void of you forming into a blackhole from the sheer density of your mind, of your thoughts, of your stupidity and carelessness in love. take the square root of this and then divide by the radius you put between us. we live less than ten minutes away, you are on the other side of town, it was always a difficult rendezvous but it was always worth it, and add in the distance you kept piling up as you became more and more careless, as you became less and less like the person i fell in love with, it is truly heartbreaking. this escape velocity is incomprehensible, i need help leaving.

light travels ninety-two million nine-hundred-sixty thousand miles
from the sun to the earth at a constant speed of about three-hundred
million meters per second. the distance between your soul and mine
is a mere three inches away and the light in your soul shines so
brightly, who knows how fast it travels // you die twice: part ii

if the sun were ever to die, the world would not know for seven
minutes. imagine turning a light switch off and having to wait seven
minutes until darkness comes. in other words, the distance between
the earth and the sun is so enormous, and the speed of light is so slow
in comparison, it would have to travel seven minutes to reach us. so
the light we would see for seven minutes after the sun went out
would be the light from the past.
now, take a step back and look at the nighttime sky. most of the
lights speckled like drops of rain are actually light from the past that
is still travelling in photons to only be interrupted by our eyes. so
when we wish on stars, we are wishing on the past, we are wishing
on stars that are probably grand light years away and are probably
long dead, but the emptiness of light has not reached our eyes yet.
now you. how long did the light in your soul take to reach me?
barely any. the second your path dared to mingle with mine by
chance, by the roll of dice, by the haphazardness in the grand scheme
of life, i was immediately blinded by the brightness surrounding your
body in an aura. and the shadows you cast surrounding you all
seemed to be elongated to the point of never making a definite shape.
your soul is so bright i am glad i got to be a part of the journey you
call life because i got to see the brightness in its full budding
capacity. you told me you learned that you were sick of being the
shadows of other people so you made yourself your own sun.
the photons from your soul were never interrupted, they were too
beautiful to interrupt.
most people are not as budding as you are when it comes to the
emission of lights. most people are weak, their shine is dull. but you,
you are a different story. you are beautiful, you are light.
and even if one day that light decides to burn out, and even if one
day the distance between your body and mine is not the three inches
separating us on this bed, and even if the sun dies and the light takes
seven minutes to travel to us, and even if the light we see in the sky
is light from millions of years ago, i know for sure this holds true:
your soul is so bright, it will never, ever, truly burn out.

PE=mgh

potential energy is defined as the energy that is stored by an object
when it is in any given position:
further defined, potential energy is the mass of an object multiplied
by its height, in meters, multiplied again by the constant nine-point-
eight meters per second of gravity.
the potential energy of you and i when we were together was so high:
our mass was both of our weight put together, both of our heavy
minds and souls.
multiplied by gravity, the constant.
and we fell in love from a height which scraped the stars, a height
which made my knees grow weak with fear, fear of falling, fear of
never coming back, a height in which no one could reach.
but our potential energy
is now kinetic.
and it is amazing.

the breaking point

i think schools
should change their curriculum.
especially for science.
because in physics i learned
that anything with mass
has a center of gravity:
a point where if the base of the body
extends far enough past it,
the body will fall.
yet our minds
have breaking points
but no amount
of chemical formulas,
mathematical background,
or even physics
could describe the point
at which
all the weight
kept on the mind
becomes too much
and we reach
our
break-
ing
point.

the planets and our love

mercury, venus,
earth and then mars;
i would look at you
like stargazers at stars.

jupiter, saturn,
uranus and then neptune;
i needed you
like earth and the moon.

pluto, nebulas,
quasars and then galaxies;
like the tides of the ocean
i thought we would never cease.

galaxies, quasars,
nebulas and then pluto;
who was i to know
you would be the one to go?

neptune, uranus,
saturn and then jupiter;
my heart poured out from my sleeve
and you were the murderer.

mars, earth,
venus and then mercury;
our heartbreak and the planets' order:
some things that were meant to be.

the dark side of the moon and of me and of you

we were etched into supernovas
and written in all of the stars;
our love was beyond celestial,
bigger than jupiter, mightier than mars.

we were the dark matter
and the brightness of the galaxies;
we were the rings of saturn
and the planet with frozen seas.

we were the start of all of earth's creation,
and the wavelengths in outer space;
we were the light of all of the quasars,
yet the gravity that held everything in place.

but we are now the wake of black holes,
and this is the dark side of the moon;
our love once was beyond celestial
but i guess you and i have a darker side too.

universe, unified

his eyes
held expansive
novels
and hers
formed poetry;
their love
was art
with a
wonderful
legacy.

her heart
was a star
but his
was a
black hole
they were the
universe
with one
true
soul.

oxygen

some scientists believe that oxygen is highly toxic and that the entire
human population and all of the other species that cover the earth die
in a certain span of years because that is how long it takes for the
oxygen to kill them. divergently, other scientists are not skeptics and
believe natural causes are the reason of death and that oxygen is the
pure source of life.
either way: with, or without oxygen, you are dead.
i guess all i am trying to say:
you are my oxygen.

entanglement

him: "the theory of entanglement is the idea that if two particles are created at the same time, if two electrons were born at the exact same moment in the continuum of time and space, they are connected: if you turn one of them clockwise, the other immediately turns counterclockwise. and this can happen over hundreds of thousands of light years. what entanglement also states is that since the big bang created every single thing, every single thing is also connected."

he pauses, looks around at the room, finds his way through the library with his eyes. we are in my favorite section, and his least favorite. the love stories. the sappy romances filled with images of fictitious futures. my favorite.

him: "this explains you and me. this explains everything we have been through. this explains that somehow, by some act of God—no, something greater, an act of scientific chances, probability and equations: i found you. i found this imperfect human being who was perfect for me. i found someone i love and someone i adore. i found someone whose name is lavender kisses and whose soul is bright. i found someone who takes me to the moon in my dreams and to the stars every day. i found someone. i found you."

man, oh man, how i do love every single aspect about him. he knows the name of the connectivity between electrons and neutrons, and every other scientific thing i might ever need to know. he has a soul of true stardust and he says that the amount of stars in the sky is not even close to the amount of things he loves about me, but if those were the same number, it would never get dark. i love him. i love him. i love him so much.

him: "i guess we were connected from the moment we stepped onto this earth. every single thing i have done, every single heartbreak i have painstakingly gone through, every single thing i dare to call a mistake, brought me to you. this entire time i thought my conscience was talking to me, but entanglement says that we have been connected. maybe you were talking to me, leading me to you through scientific theories about the universe and reasoning brought upon by nothing but human impulsivity."

my mind was racing with images of love and our future and the day that we met: in the library, in this library right here. he was looking for a book on physics for the new class he has to teach in the college he works in and i was here looking for some new love-y dove-y reads. and he told me that the book i was holding, some john green book, was amazing. he later told me that he hated love stories. and i was busting his ass when i asked him "what about the john green book?" and he said, "if i am being honest, i had not read it until after we met. i just needed to make small talk with this beautiful girl that was standing by me. and i am so glad our relationship began on a throne of lies." he laughed, "but i did read it the day after. i read every last page of it. and i have to say, it was pretty damn good. sappy and gross, yes. but good, nonetheless."

him: "entanglement says that we are connected. but so do our bodies. so do our souls."

and then i thought of our first date when he took me out to a fancy restaurant and accidentally spilled his soup. so we left and went to some fast food restaurant. and when he dropped me off he said that was the best and worst first date and i said that it was the best. and he kissed me goodnight and when i got inside i was smiling like i was living in that fucking john green book i got him to read and it seemed like my life was perfect.

him: "i never thought i would meet someone like you. but i absolutely adore you. i love you. and i want to spend every waking moment, every single second and nanosecond attempting to memorize the back of your hand and the inside of your heart and mind. i want to spend every single day trying to make my heart fall more and more for you. i want you to be mine forever. i want our life to be a story in this section."

he bent down on one knee, pulled something out of his back pocket and asked the question i had been dying to hear:

him: "will you marry me?"

fall in love with physicists. they know the intermingled-ness between love and physics.

part ten;

the loving, hurting, dying, resurrection, and haunting of me, you, and us

the difference between love and loss: part i

i did not
know
what it
meant
to be in love
but i knew
for sure
this is what
it felt like
to be broken.

liking and enjoying

i
think my
new favorite color
is the color of your lips,
and i am dying to
know what
shade
would be
created when our
lips finally decide to mix;
you said your lips
craved me
but
obviously
since then your
taste and your palate
has changed, you said you
loved me but had
"no time at
all" to
explain.

it only takes a spark to start a wildfire

honestly

who

knew

you were

a spark

and i

was

detonative.

i used to hold a heart that was semipermeable

but you made it lock completely.

you were a supernova when i met you.
i did not know that meant the beginning of the death of a star.

i

drew

constell-

ations

in

the

words

you

said

to

me

but

dear

god

did

they

turn

into

such

black

holes.

i gave you my all, you left, and now i have nothing

i am so sorry
i was only able
to give you
the light from
a dimly lit star
when you
deserved the
light
of a thousand
vibrant suns.

the saddest thing anyone has ever told me

at my funeral

make sure

it is

a closed casket.

i do not

want people

to see

how happy

i have

become.

she does not really dance anymore

every single night
she danced to the beat
of his evergreen heart
but she found it hard
to keep a steady beat
with a metronome
broken from the start.

love and loss: part ii

it was
at that point—

when i was not
worried about
the future
and where
we would be in twenty years

but trying
to picture
a life without you
and i was not
able to—

i realized that i will love you
undoubtedly,
fully,
exceptionally,
and most importantly
forever.

i used to see you in all of the stars in the sky
but now everything is black

but it is safe to say
like you, my color is
completely and utterly gone;
faded like an
uninteresting sunrise
at the brink of dawn.

i am still breathing
but i am the furthest
from ever being
alive;
and although
my heart is beating
i will never
truly survive.

tattoos reside
on all the strings
of my heart
they remind me of when
you were here;
but the
ink never fades
and my memory
will never
disappear.

i am destructive

i seem to
extinguish
every single fire
i inaugurate.

there is a difference between being problematic and you; the latter of which is worse

you were
hydrophobic,
and nothing
but irresolute;
and though
you had
anthrophobia,
all you created
on me
were roots.

you were
a kleptomaniac,
and took
pills for
your calamity;
you were
a hypochondriac,
but you still
said that
"your biggest
problem
was me."

lonely but not alone

i am lonely, yes,
but certainly, i am not alone;
like a king inside an empty castle
sitting on the throne.

like a sailor with no wind,
a dreamer with nothing to dream;
i am stressed, depressed
and everything in between.

or a candle with no flame,
an artist with nothing for a medium;
i am a musician
with no sense of rhythm.

like i am hurting myself and helping others,
a black firestone.
i am lonely, yes,
but certainly, i am not alone.

the opposite of love is emptiness, not hate

and there is no light
without any such form
of darkness.

and there is no good
without anything that
is evil.

and i think there is not love
without first feeling
something like
loss.

love and loss: part iii

i do not love you
he said
i am in love with you
he finished
and it is quite sad, really, because
you mean the world to me,
everything about you means the
absolute world to me,
but it probably means nothing for you.
i am probably
just a speck, an atom,
while you are
the entire galaxy,
the entire universe,
and i do not think
you realize just how in love with you i am
i go to sleep and i am thinking about you
and then when i wake up
you are still the only thing on my mind.
and you know the saying
if you are awake past one in the morning
you are either in love or lonely?
he paused and ran his fingers through his brown hair
i think i am both.

acknowledgements // outro

so first of all i want to thank anyone who may have inspired a little truth out of these pieces. i want to thank anyone who made me feel happy and caused me to write something. to anyone who made me feel sad and made me write something. to anyone who made me so angry there was nothing i could do but punch the keyboard until some notion formed.

second, i want to thank my family and my closest friends. you supported me all the way through this. mom and dad, i am crazy, i know, and i know, i know, i should find something that can one day support a family BUT LOOK I JUST PUBLISHED A BOOK I WILL WORRY ABOUT MY FUTURE IN THE FUTURE, but nonetheless i love you guys so much. thank you for always supporting me. dad, without you this would not have been possible. all of your editing and comments on which pieces you liked best had me smiling each time i went through to edit. thank you for giving your time to help me. my sisters, sarah and delilah, thank you just for being you guys. crazy and understanding. and lilah, thank you for giving me rhyming words or just listening to what i had to say even when you literally wanted nothing to do with me. sarah, you are my late-night inspiration. my best friend, mikayla. thank you for making me want to do this. for pushing me even when i thought i could not go any further. thank you for talking to me on nights when i did not know what to do and guiding me every single step of the way.

third, thank you to my school/town. like honestly, there are some people in this town that i absolutely adore. i do not know if i should really name names, but you know who you are. (naming three people who deserve it: jamie m, danielle s, and sabrina k, you guys are boss). when you comment on my pictures i literally die a little bit inside. and to those people who talked to me at homecoming about my account (and were seniors when i was a freshmen), thank you for telling me i was awesome. i really needed to hear that. i live in an amazing town full of some pretty amazing people and i cannot thank you guys enough.

fourth, thank you to all of my [english] teachers, especially mr. kokum (he is the one who now teaches zumba), ms. scarpelli (plane crash story), ms. guida/alamo (not my english teachers, just awesome people who shaped me to be me and wrote poetry with me), mr. johnston (my eighth grade teacher, i aspire to become you), ms. dono (ninth grade english teacher, you are awesome), ms. lemire (tenth grade english teacher, equally as awesome), and mrs. rainone (my eleventh grade teacher who lit a new, better, brighter spark underneath me with my writing).

also, thank you to my friends: michaela s (who wanted to be stated as perfect...but i have other ideas) for being there all the time and tolerating my ratchetness, alexa s (you have been there since day one of my first account and i can not even begin to use the words to describe how thankful i am to have you), bella m (even though i never text you back, i love you), the daly twins, and anyone i am forgetting. even if we don't talk much anymore, i would be nowhere without you. and i mean that. you got me to where i am today.

and a very special thank you to danni r, my cousin, you are my girl, my number one, and my cp/ft instead of nf/chill. where would i be if not for you?

thank you to my fam i met through instagram and throwback to all of those fun group chats. mainly thank you to: alexa (sexi lexi), kai (kai so fly), lauren (a banana and a cat), kat (give me your discounts), angel (my band fam), leo (you have the best hair), nash (my brother), julia (hulia hoop), zoe (zoeeeeee or mom), vic (my og), and all the other people i am too tired to mention (including audrey #humanbean).

BUT MAINLY THANK YOU TO MY HOMIE TAYLOR SWIFT. I WOULD BE NOWHERE WITHOUT YOU/THAT GIRL. THANK YOU TAYLOR FOR INSPIRING ME IN COUNTLESS WAYS. YOU ARE AMAZING. YOU ARE THE REASON I DO WHAT I DO. THANK YOU (did you expect this because my biggest dream in life is literally having taylor sign right here...)

X_____

most importantly: thank you. thank you for reading this. thank you for buying this. thank you for listening. i would be nowhere if it was not for you.

without you i am just some emo boy writing poetry.

you have given me a purpose the past five years of my life. you have given me a reason. a spark. you have given me a life. a dream. you have taken everything within me and you have read my mind, pieced together the pieces of myself that i thought were gone. you have created me. you have watched me grow, struggle, find myself, lose myself, become myself. you have supported me when i thought i had no one. thank you to anyone who comments on my posts the kindest things, who direct messages me and tells me something. i know i do not always reply but you guys are at the center of it all. thank you. i really do love you guys.

if a poem touches you, let me know; if these words resonate with you, reach out to me; if you need someone to talk to, my ears are always there for your use. i know what it is like to love, i know how hard it is to hurt; i am you, and you are me.

and know that this will be the first one of many...

noah roselli
@nr.poems
/n.r/

about the author

noah roselli is sixteen years old and is about to be a senior in high school. he spends his days usually writing on Instagram, connecting with friends, or relaxing with the rest of his family. with college fast approaching, noah wishes to major in physics with a concentration in either astronomy or engineering, but wholeheartedly is never giving up writing.
he loves dogs, taylor swift, seltzer, and connecting with people, whether it be through his account or through people in his hometown.

Made in the USA
Middletown, DE
19 December 2017